THE PSYCHOLOGY OF EFFECTIVE MANAGEMENT

The Psychology of Effective Management combines basic psychological principles with practical recommendations for building positive and productive manager–employee relations. Each recommendation is based on real-life situations taken from respected scholars in the field, as well as the author's own professional experiences. With particular attention to the human element of management, the practical advice presented in this book is aimed at helping managers create a positive psychological environment in the workplace and lead their employees into a productive and satisfying professional life. The content is presented in an easy-to-follow format so that any manager can put his or her knowledge immediately into practice. By striking a compelling balance between the science and practice of management, this will be an indispensable resource for managers, administrators, and business owners at all levels as well as students of business and management.

Fred Voskoboynikov is an American citizen who emigrated from the former Soviet Union. He completed graduate and postgraduate programs in Social Psychology at Leningrad University (now St. Petersburg University, Russia). Since immigrating to the United States, he has worked as a manager of construction projects in San Francisco and the surrounding areas. He previously worked as an industrial psychologist in a civil engineering firm and taught ergonomics and the psychology of management at Civil Engineering University in Odessa, Ukraine.

THE PSYCHOLOGY OF EFFECTIVE MANAGEMENT

Strategies for Relationship Building

Fred Voskoboynikov

Taylor & Francis Group
NEW YORK AND LONDON

First published 2017
by Routledge
711 Third Avenue, New York, NY 10017

and by Routledge
2 Park Square, Milton Park, Abingdon, Oxon, OX14 4RN

Routledge is an imprint of the Taylor & Francis Group, an informa business

© 2017 Taylor & Francis

The right of Fred Voskoboynikov to be identified as author of this work has been asserted by him in accordance with sections 77 and 78 of the Copyright, Designs and Patents Act 1988.

All rights reserved. No part of this book may be reprinted or reproduced or utilised in any form or by any electronic, mechanical, or other means, now known or hereafter invented, including photocopying and recording, or in any information storage or retrieval system, without permission in writing from the publishers.

Trademark notice: Product or corporate names may be trademarks or registered trademarks, and are used only for identification and explanation without intent to infringe.

© Illustrations by David Puketza

Library of Congress Cataloging in Publication Data
Names: Voskoboynikov, Fred, author.
Title: The psychology of effective management : strategies for relationship building / Fred Voskoboynikov.
Description: 1 Edition. | New York : Routledge, 2017. | Includes bibliographical references and index.
Identifiers: LCCN 2016025033 | ISBN 9781138655577 (hardback : alk. paper) | ISBN 9781138655584 (pbk. : alk. paper) | ISBN 9781315511290 (ebook)
Subjects: LCSH: Management.
Classification: LCC HD31 .V68 2017 | DDC 658.4/094—dc23
LC record available at https://lccn.loc.gov/2016025033

ISBN: 978-1-138-65557-7 (hbk)
ISBN: 978-1-138-65558-4 (pbk)
ISBN: 978-1-315-51129-0 (ebk)

Typeset in Bembo
by Apex CoVantage, LLC

To Nina, Maya, and Daniel

CONTENTS

Preface		ix
Prologue		xi
1	The Significance of Human Factors	1
	From the History of Motivation in Industry 2	
	Humans Under the Magnifying Glass of Sciences 4	
	Work Physiology and Work Psychology 6	
	Industrial/Organizational Psychology 7	
	Engineering Psychology and Ergonomics 8	
	Social Psychology 10	
2	What We Have in Common and What Makes Us Different	13
	Activity Theory on the Development of the Human Mind 13	
	We All are "Custom Made" 16	
	The Temperament Question 18	
	Temperament and the Features of the Nervous System 21	
	Let's Characterize Character 25	
3	Personality Features and Performance	31
	Nature vs. Nurture: Is It Worth Debating? 31	
	Human Abilities and Activity 36	
	The Individual Style of Activity 43	

| 4 | What's Going on in Groups? | 49 |

     People Need People 49
     Small and Large Social Groups 52
     Formal and Informal Groups and Social Roles 54
     The Compatibility Factor 59
     Social and Professional Adaptation and Psychological
        Security 66

| 5 | Management Is Like Conducting an Orchestra | 74 |

     Managing Is Your Job 74
     They Want Good Bosses 82
     The Power of Words 90
     Communication Is the Key 94
     Good Managers Are Good Listeners 101

| 6 | Additional Considerations | 105 |

     About Incompetence 105
     A Brief Introduction to Negotiating 109
     The Stress Factor 115
     A Few Business Tips 119

| 7 | Your Image Is in Your Hands | 130 |

     Factors to Pay Attention To 130
     A Moving Target Is Harder to Hit 133

| 8 | Learn to Control Yourself: 51 Illustrated Psychological Recommendations for Optimizing Manager–Employee Relations | 140 |

Index   *155*

PREFACE

Each and every one of us, consciously or unconsciously, tries to manage other people's activity to a certain degree. Managers at professional and industrial settings, business owners and plant supervisors, commanders of military units, educators, coaches of athletic teams, parents, and others—all these people fall into the category of managers by their functions. Regardless of the type of organization and the field of activity, general managerial functions are similar. In fact, management functions are considered to be universal. Managers plan and organize, coordinate, and control; make decisions and handle physical, informational, and financial resources; create and communicate, motivate and reward, and so on.

Most of attention in any organization is directed toward achieving financial goals, that is, toward profitability. That is vital for the organization and well understood. However, particularly for this reason, people's interests are not often on the priority list in organizations' affairs. If that is the case, sooner or later such an approach will backfire and prevent the organization from functioning successfully in the long run. Regardless of how "intelligent" the technology is and how the society progresses, humans always play a leading role in the functions of organizations. There are already fully automated plants where robots perform all technical operations. However, all of it takes place under people's control. Technicians come periodically; they turn the robots off and check whether there is a need for any necessary adjustments, and so on. Even if robots themselves signal what adjustments or repairs are needed, people are still the ones who monitor the needed repairs and adjustments. In pilots' activity, for example, in the case of a system failure, the manual controls need to be used in takeoff and landing. In other words, machines and materials cannot "work" without people's involvement. Hence directing all possible efforts toward creating a positive psychological environment in the workplace is of significant importance. To create such an environment without basic knowledge of psychology does not seem possible. To know people's individual characteristics, their ability to work in a group environment, as well as their values, goals, and desires is just as necessary for managers as possessing the technical knowledge in their chosen field of activity.

In the book, we present an overview of the basic psychological knowledge not as a "freestanding" theoretical presentation but as an applicable tool in combination with real-world examples and practical recommendations for building positive and productive manager–employee relations. The offered recommendations rely upon real-life situations taken from respected scholars in the field, as well as from the author's personal experience. Some recommendations are given throughout the course of the text, while others are brought together in the last chapter as a consolidation of the described material. However, as it goes without saying, making recommendations for all situations that occur in the multifaceted managerial activity does not seem possible. That is obvious and does not need to be explained. It is more important to apply the psychological knowledge in the process of managing people's activity.

Chapters and topics of the chapters are arranged in a certain logical sequence. Some topics may seem somewhat theoretical; they may be viewed at first and then, if desired, returned to later. Topics of the book include the human factors, the activity theory, and the psychology of individual differences, the effect of personality features on performance, group dynamics, psychological compatibility, specifics of managerial activity, communication, and other considerations such as the stress factor, the basics of negotiation, and the ways of creating a positive image.

The book can be regarded as a popular tutorial and, as such, should be perceived as an initial incentive and a starting point for implementing the psychological knowledge into the practice of management. From the more optimistic approach, though, the information presented in the book and the offered recommendations will hopefully do their part in helping managers to create a positive psychological environment in the workplace and in leading their people into a productive and satisfactory professional life.

The book is addressed to lower- and middle-management-level managers in various fields, but it is designed with a wide range of readers in mind. We believe that the book will be well received by students of business and management, by business owners, and by all those who wish to expand their repertoire of psychological knowledge and techniques for improving the efficiency of their activity and for maintaining mental health. To put it in a humorous mode, this book is of interest only to those ... who communicate with others.

PROLOGUE

You can be effective in management . . . if you agree that managing people at work is not a part of the management process; managing people at work *is* the management as a whole. Regardless of the area of specialization, managers work with people. A bank manager does not manage computers, safes and accounts; a construction site manager does not manage machines and equipment; a basketball coach does not manage game tactics and techniques; a ship captain does not work the steering wheel but nevertheless gets to the desired destination by managing the ship's crew. Managers manage people!

> You have to be absolutely straight with people, not clever or cute, and you can't think that you can manipulate them. That does not mean you have to think they are all stars or that you have to agree with everything they do, but the relationship, I think, ought to be real.
>
> *Don Richey, former Lucky stores CEO (as cited in Bennis, 2003)*

You can be effective in management . . . if you agree that in order to achieve success in working with people, possessing only the technical knowledge of your profession is not enough. You can be highly technical in your field, you can be good with numbers, marketing, and other things, but if you lack people skills, it will become a predicament in the process of implementing your managerial functions.

Universities, unfortunately, are not always the best place to learn. Too many of them are less places of higher learning than they are high-class vocational schools. Too many produce narrow-minded specialists who may be wizards at making money, but who are unfinished as people. These specialists have been taught how to do, but have not learned how to be.

Warren Bennis, the author of On Becoming a Leader

You can be effective in management ... if you agree that to achieve success in managing people in the long run, you have to be able to project a positive image; you have to be able to motivate others to perform with enthusiasm.

Up to a point, I think you can lead out of fear, intimidation, as awful as that sounds. You can make people follow you by scaring them, and you can make people follow by having them feel obligated. [...] The person following has to believe that following is the best thing to do at the time. [...] You don't want people to follow you just because that's what they're paid for.

Sydney Pollack, Academy Award–winning film director, producer, actor, and writer (as cited in Bennis, 2003)

You can be effective in management ... if you agree that one person can do the work of one person. Managers achieve success by the success of their people. You have to be able to build a strong team where each member can use his or her best abilities and has the opportunity to grow professionally. You have to be able to delegate the right tasks to the right people. This way, you will get the best of what people are capable of, and they will experience their importance.

Successful people use their strength by recognizing, developing and utilizing the talents of others.

Ben Stein, economist, lawyer, and writer

You can be effective in management ... if you recognize individual differences in people and apply this knowledge in the process of management; if you take the group dynamic into account and its influence on people's performance. You can practice the following philosophy: People come to work to perform, where there is no place for "tender loving care" and where their performance is demanded regardless. However, the fact that you are dealing with people and not with robots remains—people with their unique individuality, their principles and values, and their goals and expectations. Ignoring these factors will prevent you from creating a positive psychological atmosphere in the workplace and accessing their full capacity.

Situations taking place in business almost always have to do with situations of relations among people. Managers with perfect sense to understand people's psychology and readiness to apply this knowledge become successful in business.

Mark McCormack, the author of What They Don't Teach You at Harvard Business School

You Can Be Effective in Management!

References

Bennis, W. (2003). *On Becoming a Leader*. New York: Basic Books.
McCormack, M. H. (1986). *What They Don't Teach You at Harvard Business School*. New York: A Bantam Book.

1

THE SIGNIFICANCE OF HUMAN FACTORS

Humans are surrounded by different kinds of environments. Air temperature, noise, and lighting are elements of physical environment. Machines, mechanisms, and the like make for a technical environment. People surrounding humans at work constitutes a social environment. Humans, as biological creatures, have a high degree of adaptability to the surrounding environment and are able to function under a fairly wide range of different conditions. People can work quite productively for a relatively long period of time in conditions of low and high temperatures, in conditions of excessive noise, under poor lighting, and so on. Our body constantly reacts to the changing temperature of the environment and by thermoregulatory processes keeps a comfortable body temperature. Our hearing adapts to the level of sounds and noises. Our eyes adapt to objects located at different distances in the field of vision by the accommodation of the lens. Humans can work productively in an uncomfortable body position, in conditions of time limits and danger, in conditions of subordinating their actions to the regimens of the machines and mechanisms that they operate. The same applies to the social environment. If the social environment evokes negative emotions, people can still perform productively by suppressing negative emotions. However, the degree of adaptation to the surrounding environment in which humans can function without immobilizing the body systems has its limitations. Continuous work in such conditions sooner or later will have a negative impact on human health. Thus the question is not whether people can adapt to the stressful environment and continue to perform but to what level this adaptation is possible without harming their physical and mental being. In other words, what price do people pay, physiologically and psychologically, for such adaptation? In this regard, creating an optimal working environment may not only increase productivity but will have a positive effect on people's health and longevity.

From the History of Motivation in Industry

Pioneers of the Employee Motivation Movement

The early figures who planted the seeds for the employee motivation movement were British reformer Robert Owen and Scottish doctor Andrew Ure.[1] Robert Owen was one of the first to recognize the importance of human resources and the human needs of employees. Owen is considered a man ahead of his time. Until his era, factory workers were generally viewed much as appendages to machines and equipment. Being a factory owner himself, he improved working conditions for his workers. During his lifetime, he endeavored to improve the health, education, well-being, and rights of the working class. Many of his views are relevant today in their translation to our modern times. Andrew Ure also was a proponent of a humanistic approach to employees' needs and providing workers with good working conditions. He introduced the human factors as an additional aspect of manufacturing, along with the mechanical and commercial ones. Unfortunately, the attempts of these two pioneers to improve working conditions were not picked up and developed by others. Workers at plants and factories worked long hours under intolerable conditions. Much of manufacturing work was piecework; that is, workers were paid per unit produced. The only method used to motivate workers for better performance was to offer more money.

The Scientific Management Theory

Under the impact of the Industrial Revolution of 1820–1870 and the pressure of growing competition, plants and factories' owners were looking for ways to increase productivity of labor. In the early 1900s came Frederick W. Taylor, who is considered the earliest advocate of scientific management and who played the dominant role in it in his time. In 1881, he proposed the Scientific Management Theory as a way of making the conduct of work-related activities more efficient. He described his method in *The Principles of Scientific Management* (1911). The major postulate of the theory was an assumption that individual workers would be willing to work hard for monetary rewards. Taylor introduced wage incentives schemes so that workers could get paid more for increased production. Taylor insisted that workers will be satisfied by this motivational method and that the cost per unit will be reduced.

Workers adapted to the scientific management method positively, and, as a result, productivity was significantly increased. The Scientific Management Theory was taken as some kind of an industrial panacea of the time. History showed, however, that this method of scientific management worked to a certain point. With increased productivity, many owners changed the production standards. That is, the same incentives that gave workers the opportunity to have higher pay hit them hard afterward. Workers realized that "every stick has two ends." When the productivity exceeded market demand, it led to job insecurity and to temporary layoffs. That, in turn, led to hostility between workers and employers. Hidden sabotage and damage of the equipment was workers' response to the administration's "tightening the screws," that is, increasing production norms for the same pay. Thus scientific management began to encounter failures.

Despite the fact that wages are still considered the main motivating factor for increasing productivity, motivation by only economic incentives works for a certain period of time. People see more than just earnings in their work; they also work for reasons other than money. They are filled with thoughts and ideas and want to see them implemented, along with receiving monetary rewards. By the early 20th century, many voices were against Taylor's scientific management.

The Beginning of the Psychology of Management

Many psychological researchers of that time, both in the United States and other countries, criticized Taylor's method because it suggested treating people as machines. One of the earliest authors who instigated the psychological aspects of scientific management was Lillian Gilbreth (1914), an engineer and industrial psychologist. In 1914, she, together with her husband Frank Gilbreth, a pioneer of motion study, formed their own form of scientific management, which focused on the human element in management. In her book *The Psychology of Management: The Function of the Mind in Determining, Teaching, and Installing Methods of Least Waste*, written the same year (1914), Lillian Gilbreth incorporated concepts of human relations and worker individuality into management principles. It was a major early work in the field of industrial psychology and scientific management. In the book, she expressed the view that scientific management should be built on the principle of recognition of the individual, not only as an economic unit but as a personality, stressing the importance of including the human element in management. For the first time in history, the basic elements of management theory were brought together, including the knowledge of individual behavior, the theory of groups, the theory of communication, and a rational basis for decision making.

The Birth of the Human Relations Movement

Taylor's scientific management was soon replaced by the Human Relations Movement, proposed by Harvard sociologist Elton Mayo and his colleagues. In the 1920s, Mayo was invited to study jobs at a Philadelphia textile mill after the hired experts unsuccessfully tried to implement Taylor's scientific management, which only increased the turnover. Mayo made a simple observation that the problem was the result of the monotony of the work. He suggested allowing the workers to take periodical breaks during the working shifts among his other suggestions. The sharp decrease of turnover was a pleasant surprise for the management. In 1928, Mayo conducted a series of experiments at Western Electric.

A group of six women workers were selected based on their preference to work together and placed to work in a separate room. Such an environment allowed the experimenter to change the conditions of the experiment whenever needed. The women participated in decisions regarding the changes in the experiments' conditions. They were allowed to take additional breaks during the shift; they had shorter working hours, free lunches, and some other incentives. In other words, they did not feel like "slaves rowing in a galley" but rather felt elevated to some elite status. As a result, their productivity jumped tremendously. The most interesting thing happened after all favorable conditions were removed. In spite of such a drastic and intentional deterioration of physical and material conditions, their productivity remained quite high. Mayo established that these six women unconsciously formed some tight psychological connections, helped one another, and became friends, that is, they created *informal* relations within the *formal* group. This experiment was the beginning phase in studying human relations.

If Taylor saw the worker as a separate individual whose only goal was to get better pay, Mayo suggested a human relations approach in management. His experiments showed that the worker is not a simple tool but a complex personality interacting in a group situation that was hard to deal with and thoroughly misunderstood. The Mayo experiments at Western Electric have gone down in history as classical in the study of motivation in industry. Described in terms of modern psychological language, Mayo's experiments demonstrated the importance of taking the human element into account in the process of management. It's worth noting, however, that despite the criticism that Taylor's scientific management theory has undergone, he was the first one to call attention to the search for production efficiency.

Humans Under the Magnifying Glass of Sciences

The Impact of Technological Progress on Humans

The incredible technological progress of the last century, especially since World War II, has changed the nature of human activity dramatically. All the significant achievements of modern civilization have transformed how humans collaborate with humans. Technical links have wedged between man and the object of labor. That, in turn, gradually and steadily put more weight on mental processes such as perception, concentration of attention, memorization, thinking, decision making, and the like, while the proportion of heavy physical efforts decreased. Technological progress has brought new, previously unknown occupational hazards: informational stress, intellectual strain, sensory and motor monotony, allergenic habitats, lack of exercise, and more.

The state of the organism changes with activity, which is characterized by the cost of internal resources to a certain degree. If the cost is too high, it becomes a real threat to human health. The reason for the increasing cost of internal resources lies in the inadequacy of modern technology to accommodate the physiological and psychological capabilities of humans, as well as the rapid variability of forms of collective cooperation and social communication. The same applies to the micro social environment. If the social environment projects a positive influence, the work process flows with the background of positive emotions and is more productive. The negative social environment evokes an undesirable emotional state, which negatively influences both productivity and human health.

In theoretical medicine, the health of a population is considered an indicator of the nation's well-being, as a factor that has a direct impact on the productivity and overall economic performance of the society. This integrated approach is reflected in the definition of health from the World Health Organization (WHO) as "a state of complete physical, mental and social well-being" and not merely the absence of diseases. That is, it should be looked at not only from the medical perspective but from the psychological perspective as well because it involves the reaction of the individual to the impact of adverse factors. Whenever there is an excessive reaction of the organism to stressors, the neurotic syndromes of pathological, emotional, or psychosomatic problems take place. These disorders adversely influence not only individuals but also their families. People's psychological health is one of the basic criteria for the social stability of every individual and society as a whole.

Fields of Science Studying Human Activity

The accomplishments of the applied fields of science studying human activity—such as work physiology and work psychology, industrial/organizational psychology, social psychology, engineering psychology, and ergonomics—are a powerful force in creating better quality of people's life. Physiological and psychological studies are conducted for the purpose of determining the influence of various environmental factors (light, noise, temperature, etc.), for the design features of machinery and equipment, for ascertaining the effects of monotony, working posture, and many other conditions on such human characteristics as perception, attention, thinking, reaction speed, precision movements, and so on. The purpose of these studies is to create an optimal working environment, to improve the quality of work, to increase safety, to reduce and eliminate emergency situations, and so on. All of that positively influences workers' mental and physical state and their satisfaction with the work process. The study of the physiological and psychological capabilities of human activity and integrating this knowledge into practice help create an optimum environment for people in the workplace with the purpose of increasing productivity and preserving human health.

Before briefly considering these relatively new (in the history of humankind) fields of study of human activity, it should be noted that all of them are closely intertwined, and some of the names are often used interchangeably. For example, industrial psychology is sometimes used to describe work psychology, ergonomics as human factors, and so on. Although the work in the respective fields somewhat differs, there are some similarities between them. But the most important thing is that these fields of science share same objectives, which are to optimize the effectiveness and efficiency of human activity and to improve the general quality of people's life.

Work Physiology and Work Psychology
Humans and Tools

Over the centuries, humans have used primitive tools for their labor activity, which were gradually changed and improved. However, for a very long time, practically until the beginning of the 20th century, human functions in relation to the use of tools and primitive machinery remained fundamentally the same. Namely, people mostly used their muscular force in manipulating tools. The harmonization of humans with tools was mainly based on consideration of anatomical (anthropometric) and physiological features of humans in designing tools. On the scientific level, the influence of the physical working environment on human performance was studied in the framework of *work physiology*. Work physiology studies physiological changes in the human organism during working activity and develops a physiological rationale of the work processes that contributes to the long-term workability at the optimal level. For example, by creating and maintaining optimum conditions of the physical environment, such as temperature, lighting, humidity, and the like, it's possible to positively affect people's performance and satisfaction with the work process.

Humans and Technology

Due to the incredible technological progress of the 19th and 20th centuries, new types of work activity emerged. Operating trains, cars, planes, and other modern machinery and technical devices required entirely new qualities from people, basically psychological, such as concentration of attention, memorization, thinking, decision making, reaction speed, and the like. To perform these kinds of activity, humans had to subordinate their actions to the working regimens of the machinery and modern technology that they control and operate. The emergence of new types of working activity led to the necessity of studying human physiological and psychological capabilities in the process of interaction with new technology. That has led to the development of a new scientific discipline—*work psychology*. Work psychology is a branch of psychology that studies the characteristics of different kinds of work in their dependence on the sociohistorical and specific production conditions, on training methods, and on the psychological qualities of people.

The purpose of physiological and psychological studies is to determine the impact of various factors of the production environment (lighting, noise, air temperature effects, etc.)—the design features of machinery and equipment, working posture, monotony factors, and others—on such human characteristics as perception, attention, thinking, reaction speed, precise movements, and so forth. These factors affect workers' state, their mood, and their satisfaction with the work process, which in turn have an effect on performance and human health. Creating optimal hygienic and aesthetic norms of the work environment is also a part of such studies. These studies are necessary because even the usual working conditions that do not match psychological and physiological human capabilities result in a higher cost of mental and physical energy.

Industrial/Organizational Psychology

Two Branches of Industrial/Organizational Psychology (I/O Psychology)

Industrial/organizational psychology, in short, is the psychology of work. The impetus for the emergence of I/O psychology was the Industrial Revolution of 1820–1870, when factories, plants, and assembly lines began coming into existence. Owners of the industrial enterprises were looking for ways to increase productivity, and I/O psychology was born in response to that. The subject of I/O psychology is to study human behavior in organizations and to apply this knowledge to practice with the purpose of promoting the well-being of people in the workplace. It is concerned with the development and application of scientific principles to the workplace. As it says in its name, modern I/O psychology consists of two branches. The industrial branch is sometimes referred to as personnel psychology because it involves searching for ways of how best to match individuals to specific job roles. It includes human resource planning, job analysis, recruitment and selection, training, performance appraisal, and carrier development. The organizational branch of I/O psychology is more focused on understanding how organizations affect individual behavior: organizational structures, social norms, management styles, and all the other factors that can influence people's behavior within the organization.

Scientific and Applied Sides of I/O Psychology

I/O psychology is a scientific field with the purpose of developing theories and testing ideas about how people think, feel, and act at work. It is also an applied field dedicated to applying psychological principles to work settings with the goal of getting people to perform better and making their lives better so that the organizations can meet their goals. One of the first figures of the industrial psychology movement in the United States was Morris Viteles.[2] He was the first one who recognized I/O psychology not as a pure academic discipline but as a practical one as well with its application to practice. He confirmed it in his own life and work. He combined a full-time professorship and a staff position at the

Philadelphia Electric Company as Director of Personnel Research and Training. He used this dual role of the scientist-practitioner to demonstrate the effectiveness of the interaction of science and profession and of research and practice. He implemented many of his ideas in the "real" world. For example, he created a test for finding workers who would not lose control when confronted with electrical emergencies in operating electric power stations. During what appeared to be a routine test to show that the applicant could do simple operations, a 10,000-volt charge of electricity would suddenly crackle across the panel in front of the candidate. By selecting those applicants who kept calm during the test, the company reduced human errors that led to substation failures from 36 a year to five a year.

Viteles created many other tests for selecting the right people for the right jobs. He designed tests for identifying the best trolley operators, typists, stenographers, and other workers for other companies. He also was the author of the first modern book in the field of industrial psychology. The important point of Morris Viteles' legacy of his long life as an industrial psychologist is his creed: "It is important that a man be kept out of a job for which he is not fitted. It is more important that he be placed in a job where he can be efficient and happy" (as cited in Wallace, 1996). Managers should use this principle in their management practice in order to preserve people's satisfaction in the workplace and to achieve better performance.

Engineering Psychology and Ergonomics

Human Capabilities in Managing Technology

Human possibilities to perform increased greatly due to the development of modern technology, but at the same time technology is becoming increasingly complex, making it more and more difficult for humans to perform controlling functions. With the introduction of automated systems of control, the specificity of human labor has changed even more significantly. For example, a human operator of a technical system is often far from the objects that she or he controls and monitors. The process of monitoring is performed based on the signals received from devices and indicators on the control display panel. Human functions are confined more and more to intellectual operations: observation, perception and decoding of information, memorization, analysis of information, decision making, and actions. In this regard, for successful implementation, technology must be designed in harmony with the psychological and physiological human capabilities. If these factors are not taken into account, the capacity of modern technology cannot be used effectively; the work of engineers and designers will be reduced due to human errors. Most importantly, it can lead to undesirable consequences, such as accidents, loss of human lives, and other undesirable outcomes.

Before the emergence of engineering psychology, machines and mechanisms were created by engineers and designers. The role of psychologists mainly was to "find" people suitable to the new technology by a selection procedure and by developing training methods to make people better "fit" the technology. The complex task in designing the technology with a consideration of human capabilities goes beyond traditional work psychology. There is a need to study the interaction between man and technology as a single system. Since then, psychologists work with engineers and designers for the integration of the human element into the designing of technical systems. Thus, based on work psychology and technical sciences, a new direction in studying human activity at work has emerged—the science of *engineering psychology*. The object of the study in engineering psychology is the so-called "man–machine system."

In the broader sense, engineering–psychological studies are needed everywhere where machines and devices are designed for human perception, thinking, and action. Study and implementation go in both directions: through the integration of psychological and physiological capabilities of humans into designing the technology, on the one hand, and in the adaptation of humans to technology through professional selection, special training, and education, on the other hand. The important thing about the man–machine system is that the proper functioning of each component is equally important. If any of the components fails to function, it causes the entire system to fail. The following is one of the most recent examples of the lack of consideration for the human component in the man–machine system.

> In March of 2011 a pilot of an American Airlines plane called the tower to get the clearance to land, and got no answer. An air traffic controller failed to respond to two planes' request to land which were heading into Ronald Reagan Washington National Airport. He did not respond because . . . he was asleep. In a statement released by the Safety Board it says: ". . . he had been working his fourth consecutive overnight shift (10:00 p.m. to 6:00 a.m.)".
>
> *(CNN Wire Staff, 2011)*

What we can see here is that the whole work of implementing the modern technology for the safety of flights and the costs associated with it was reduced to zero. And all of this happened because of the failure of the human component in the system.

There was more than one case of air traffic controllers (at other times) falling asleep during a landing emergency. They just "forgot" that they are a component of the man–machine system and "decided" to take a nap on their own accord. Fortunately, the pilots managed to land planes without the controllers' assistance, but we cannot always rely on it. That is, the underscored concerns about the effect of fatigue on sleep-deprived controllers at work are examples of not taking the human element into account. The Federal Aviation Administration acknowledged the widespread problem with fatigue and made some changes in the air traffic controllers' work schedules. Another change the FAA implemented was to end its practice of single-staffing control towers at 26 airports and a radar facility where traffic is light between midnight and 6 a.m. They also implemented another, purely psychological method to improve the situation. As a part of the air traffic controllers' training, they are now being present in pilots' cabins, so that they can have a complete picture of how important their work is and how it helps pilots to land aircrafts safely.

Human Factors/Ergonomics

Human factors/ergonomics is broader than engineering psychology, which is specifically focused on the adaptation of equipment to people. The terms "human factors" and "ergonomics" are often used interchangeably. The International Ergonomics Association defines ergonomics as the scientific discipline concerned with the understanding of interaction among humans and other elements of a system, with the "fit" among the user, equipment, and the environment. The formation of ergonomics cannot be considered accidental. Before the advent of ergonomics, many factors of human activity have been studied by different sciences in isolation from one another. As a result, the combined effect of their studies not always provided optimal solutions. Ergonomics is an integrated science; its complex includes the applied areas of work physiology and work psychology, engineering psychology, anthropometry, biomechanics, industrial hygiene, social psychology, cognitive psychology, activity theory, some aspects of scientific organization of work, and other areas. Ergonomics does not substitute for or replace or absorb engineering psychology, work physiology, or any of the other sciences studying humans at work. By engaging in the ergonomics complex, none of them loses its autonomy.

To summarize, the tasks of ergonomics can be defined as the search for ways of adapting the new technology and the environment to humans and of adapting people's capabilities to the requirements of technology. And all of that with the goal of boosting productivity while increasing safety, reducing fatigue and stress, increasing comfort and satisfaction at the workplace, and preserving people's health and promoting their spiritual and physical development.

Social Psychology

Social psychology studies patterns of human behavior in social organizations, the relationship of people in the process of joint activities in various organized and unorganized groups. The study of the so-called "small social groups" is one of the most important areas of social psychology because, for most people, daily activity takes place in small groups—family, work crew, departmental team, school class, athletic team. Psychological phenomena in small groups include the interpersonal relationships, relationships between leader and followers in formal and informal groups, problems of psychological compatibility, and others. Creating an optimal working environment—physical, technical, hygienic, and otherwise—does not exhaust all possible influences on people's performance. Psychological problems of interpersonal relationships in the process of joint activity or a negative psychological climate in the workplace can cause more harm than poor lighting, excessive noise, and an uncomfortable working posture or difficulty in reading indicators on the display panels. The systematic impact of unfavorable factors of a sociopsychological nature can lead to conditions when the human body cannot mobilize its physiological and psychological resources in order to adapt to the increasing aggressiveness and extremes of the social environment. As a consequence, the normal functioning of regulatory and homeostatic systems can be disrupted, resulting in hidden or obvious signs of impairment.

Social psychology helps us better understand ourselves and our behavior in the process of interaction with others.

Chapter 1 in a Few Lines

1. The 20th century is the century of incredible technological and social progress.
2. The nature of human work has changed dramatically. Human work includes more and more intellectual operations, while the share of physical efforts has been reduced.
3. The problem of so-called "human factors" has emerged, which has led to the necessity of studying the physiological and psychological capabilities of humans in the process of work activity.
4. New applied fields of science studying humans at work were born: work physiology and work psychology, industrial/organizational psychology, social psychology, engineering psychology, and ergonomics.
5. The studies of the physiological and psychological capabilities of humans in activity and integrating this knowledge into practice help to create an optimum environment for people in the workplace, with the purpose of increasing productivity and preserving human health.

Notes

1 Robert Owen and Andrew Ure were the pioneers of human motivation in industry. Andrew Ure described the importance of the human factors in his book *Philosophy of Manufactures*, published in 1835.
2 Morris Viteles is considered as one of the fathers of industrial psychology. His book *Industrial Psychology*, published in 1932, was the first one in the field.

References

Cratty, C. (2011). 2 planes land at Washington Airport without controllers help. *CNN*, March 24, 2011, 9:29 a.m. EDT.

Gilbreth, L. M. (1914). *The Psychology of Management: The Function of the Mind in Determining, Teaching, and Installing Methods of Least Waste*. New York: Sturgis and Walton.

Taylor, F. W. (1911). *The Principles of Scientific Management*. New York: Harper & Brothers.

Wallace, A. (December 11, 1996). Morris Viteles, Industrial Psychologist. *Philadelphia Inquirer*.

2
WHAT WE HAVE IN COMMON AND WHAT MAKES US DIFFERENT

In the process of management, it is important to keep in mind that your perception of the world is not as it is perceived by others. Each person perceives the world through the prism of her or his unique individual personality and life experience. That often prevents us from an accurate psychological reading of other people and from perfect communication and understanding of one another. Even though people have much in common, there are no two absolutely identical people in the world. Each person is different in his or her own unique way. Some people can quickly and easily adapt to the changing environment; others are slower and not as dynamic. Some individuals can sustain tough impacts while others can't, but the latter are able to navigate in slightly noticeable changes of the surroundings that enable them to react more keenly. Some feel comfortable in performing monotonous work, while others are "falling asleep" in doing the same kind of work. Some people are happy to work in a group environment; others prefer to work on individual assignments. That is, some people are good in some things while others are good at other things. Any activity requires more than one quality of people in order for them to perform. That allows people with different qualities to adapt to the requirements of an activity by their relying on their strong qualities, thus compensating for the weaker ones and, as a result, performing equally effectively with others.

Activity Theory on the Development of the Human Mind
Activity as a Mediator

Activity theory is a theoretical framework for studying different forms of human activity. The study of personality and individual differences is a critically important area of activity theory. From the activity theory perspective, people are developed through their activity. In activity theory, special attention is given to the interrelationship of personality and activity. In activity, the subject not only changes a situation or object but also develops his or her own personality features, which are formed through activity and social interaction. Activity acts as a mediator connecting personality with the social world. That is, the psychological characteristics of the individual are not completely derived from the social environment.

Activity consists of actions that could be cognitive or internal and behavioral or external (Bedny, Karwowski and Voskoboynikov, 2010; Karwowski, Voskoboynikov and Bedny, 2012). Actions are directed toward the achievement of conscious goals. Activity can be defined as conscious, intentional, goal-oriented, and socially formed behavior that is specific to humans. Activity theory emphasizes the great difference between human and nonhuman psychic processes. The psychic processes of animals are developed according to the laws of biological evolution, whereas the psychic processes of humans are influenced by the laws of socialhistorical evolution. Work plays a huge role in the historical development of humans.

Activity Theory vs. Behaviorism

Historically, activity theory was developed in Russia in contrast to behaviorism, where American psychologist Skinner was one of the leading scientists. He introduced the concept of operant conditioning that has to do with behavior modification through positive or negative reinforcement.

Before the behavioral approach in psychology there was another method in use, the introspection method. Introspection refers to a detailed observation and recording of one's own perceptions and feelings. Skinner (1974) considered this method to be too subjective, and he was right. According to Skinner, consciousness and mental processes are not to be studied in psychology in an objective manner. Instead, Skinner concentrated on the study of external observable behavioral approaches. He attempted to use an experimental method similar to those used in physics; however, external reality in his studies was portrayed as a variety of stimuli to which a person reacts. That is, he considered humans as reactive organisms. For example, he considered thinking as a set of verbal-motor reactions, and the concept of meaning, which plays a leading role in verbal thinking, was totally ignored in his studies. This kind of approach is inappropriate in psychology because it eliminates the study of mental processes.

In 1948, the Symposium *Cerebral Mechanisms of Behavior* was held at the California Institute of Technology and is regarded by many as the end of the reign of behaviorism in psychology and the beginning of cognitive science as a formal field of study (Gardner, 1985). No more strict stimulus-response explanations of human behavior were considered acceptable. With the rise of cognitive science, human behavior was not regarded as a conditional response anymore, but rather as the ability of the human mind to explore the link between stimulus and response.

The leading Soviet scientist Rubinstein (1935) introduced the personality principal in psychology, which integrates individual and social aspects in the study of human development. According to this principal, human development is the result of the interaction of material and social practice with human subjectivity. Rubinstein's subject-oriented personality principal approach addresses inadequacies in Skinner's behavioral approach. Behaviorism ignores mediated functions of activity that provide the basis for personal development. It denies such important elements of activity as reasoning, judgment, creativity, and concept formation.

Human behavior cannot be reduced to the external stimulus–response manifestation of activity. In activity theory, a person who interacts with a situation is considered the subject; that is, we are talking about cognitive and behavioral actions rather than about the stimuli to which the subject reacts. Subjects' actions have a voluntary goal-directed character. In Skinner's approach, a conscious goal for the desired result was not considered. Rubinstein (1946) wrote that through the organization of the individual practice, society shapes the content of individual consciousness. His famous quotation "external acts through internal" emphasizes the dependence of activity on the subject's individual features. The social aspect depends on the individual, just as the individual depends on the social aspect. In the same social environment, different individuals act differently, and they are impacted by the social environment in a different way.

This brief critical analysis demonstrates that activity theory approach emerged in opposition to the behavioral approach, which dominated psychology at that time.

Self-Regulation of Activity

In activity, a person develops different strategies, which derive from the mechanisms of self-regulation. Self-regulation manifests itself through both nonconscious (*automatic*) and conscious levels (Bedny and Karwowski, 2007). At the automatic level, the conscious and verbalized aspects of self-regulation play a subordinate role. This is particularly important when imaginative and nonverbalized strategies of activity play the leading role. At the conscious level of self-regulation, the verbal and logical aspects of activity are dominant. Both levels of self-regulation are interdependent, and the relationship between them is dynamic. This interdependency gives rise to the formation of different strategies of activity that are appropriate for the external and internal conditions of activity.

At the unconscious level of self-regulation, condition unfolds as an uninterrupted process. Automotive mental operations are not organized into cognitive actions. This can be explained by the fact that the unconscious level of self-regulation is not subordinated to conscious goals. Activity is triggered automatically and performed through unconscious automotive reflective processes. The subject is conscious only of the results of this process. The conscious level of self-regulation presents itself not only as a process but also as a system of logically organized actions. Each action is organized according to mechanisms of self-regulation and has a beginning and an end. At the conscious level of self-regulation, activity can be considered a hierarchically organized system of self-regulative stages of uninterrupted reflective processes. It should be noted that psychological reflection is not a passive mirror-like reflection; it possesses active features that imply some systems of mental stages and operations. Psychological reflection is always organized as a self-regulation process. Since the process cannot be fully determined in advance, it always contains situated elements that are developed during the self-regulation process of reflection. The more complicated a person finds a task, the more important and complicated the reflective process becomes. The most complicated reflective process is thinking.

The conscious level of self-regulation is organized as a system of logically interdependent cognitive actions that are transformed one into another as activity unfolds. These actions include mental operations. The unconscious level of self-regulation unfolds as automotive unconscious operations. Psychological determination does not depend on social or external factors only but also on internal influences that are derived from the mechanisms of self-regulation. The mechanisms of self-regulation play an integrating role in the external and internal components of human activity.

Personality is developed through a person's participation in activity, which depends on the relationship between the subject and situation and the relationship between subjects; that is, activity is both internal and external.

We All are "Custom Made"

> We can't see things as they are; we see them as we are.
>
> Origin unknown

We Have a Lot in Common . . .

People have a lot of similarities, but everyone is born with a set of specific individual characteristics. That's why people are so different despite the rather "standardized" physical attributes. The human organism is a very complex biological system, its unique characteristics exclusively varied. No one has exactly the same potency for personal development. The highest value in the physical characteristic of a person in terms of its contact with the surrounding world is the brain. The higher the development of the brain is, the higher the intellectual level a person can achieve, compared to other people. The main difference of human beings from other living creatures is the ability to think abstractly, to analyze thoughts through images, and to conduct other such mental activities. The mental abilities in conjunction with the characteristics of the body give a person a wide range of possible responses based on individual thoughts, feelings, and needs in relation to the surrounding world.

In most general terms, every human being is characterized by two types of components: biological and social. Genetics is a biological or innate component of personality, whereas social is an acquired component of personality. The biological component includes physical characteristics and psychic peculiarities, which for all practical purposes do not change during the life of the individual. These include the size and body shape, height, hair and eye color, and the like. (Obviously, we exclude cases of changing physical characteristics artificially.) To the same extent, it applies to the makings, temperament, the nervous system, cognitive processes, and so on. These features are of the greatest interest to us because they manifest themselves in activity. For example, some people are quick and agile; others are slow, calm; some have a well developed logical memory; others are good at remembering things mechanically. Some have the imagination of an artist, others a type of developed abstract thinking. Generally, the individual characteristics of a person are a product of heredity, physical being, and acquired experience.

The acquired features of personality include interests, ideals, aspirations, beliefs, worldview, and the like. These features are combined under the notion of the moral characteristics of the person. Personality also changes as a result of gained experience, general knowledge, and skills, which become professional skills and habits that are formed by training. Personal characteristics and the environment define how a person will develop. The availability of a musical talent does not make one a brilliant musician unless the person dedicates his or her life to years of systematic practice. Similarly, a person can be born with excellent physical characteristics, but becoming an outstanding athlete requires devoting many years of life to training.

Personality is Unique

Each person has a unique psychological structure. There are alike people, but there are no two absolutely identical personalities: as many people as many different personalities. That's why people say that personality is unique. The social environment influences the development and formation of personality. It can be seen in the examples of identical twins. Those are the so-called "homozygote twins," which developed from one zygote that splits and forms two embryos. Homozygote twins have nearly identical biological characteristics. People say they look as much alike as two drops of water. However, their similarity is only in their appearance and dynamics of behavioral reactions. From the perspective of social qualities such as interests, beliefs, attitudes toward people, and so on, they may differ significantly from one another. The development of these different social qualities depends on the social environment in which each of them is situated.

There are many known cases where identical twins fell into different social environments and became different from each other in terms of their interaction with society. Moreover, even in the same family, twins may become very different in their social characteristics. If, for example, one of the twins gets seriously sick, parents dedicate more attention to him. This in turn may affect the development of selfish traits in him. As a result, the other twin can grow more independent, can develop leadership qualities in his relationships, while the first one will develop the quality of a follower.

Regardless of whether a person has a good or bad personality in terms of the social norms of the society, she is still a person in a psychological sense because of the acquired social and historical experience of humanity. In this sense, a criminal is also a person, but her behavior is contrary to the generally accepted social norms of the society. Thus the essence of the person is determined not by her physical being but by her social qualities.

The Temperament Question

The History of the Question

It is well-known that people react differently to the same stimuli. Think of people with whom you communicate on a daily basis, and you can easily confirm this fact. When we talk about a "short-tempered" or a "temperamental" person, we mean a person who is quick and emotional with distinct facial expressions and gestures. If another person does not clearly manifest these kinds of reactions, we say he is "even-tempered." If one person puts behind some unpleasant comments directed toward him quickly, another one won't be able to sleep well the following night and will keep dwelling on it in his mind. If one person calmly reacts to criticism, another one will "jump through the roof." His eyes, the color of his face, his body language, and other signs will display his emotional stage. That is, we can say that people react with different "psychological coloring." In essence, temperament characterizes people's behavior in terms of the force with which they respond to the same stimuli.

As mentioned, temperament and the features of the nervous system are biological features of personality and as such virtually do not change during the life of the individual. Some people, by acquiring knowledge and skills, are able to conceal their real features of temperament and the nervous system, but these kinds of behavioral reactions are "masked" reactions and are possible only in nonextreme situations. In extreme situations, in contrast, the masking of behavior acquired by life experience is diminished, and the natural qualities of the individual's temperament and the nervous system are revealed.

The word "temperament" is derived from the Latin *temperamentum*, which means the proportion or ratio. The teaching about four temperament types goes back to the ancient Greek physician Hippocrates. Indeed, Hippocrates was the first to describe the differences in people's reactions to the same stimuli. However, his teaching was not about temperament types; it was about the predominance of one of the following fluids in the organism: blood, phlegm, yellow bile, and black bile. Thus he based his teaching on a naive materialistic theory of Antiquity. Despite the fact that Hippocrates' teachings were not about temperaments but about four major fluids in the body, the names of these fluids have survived as the names of temperament types. These names are derived from Latin and Greek terms: *sanguis* (blood), *phlegma* (phlegm), *chole* (bile), and *melas chole* (black bile). Blood, "secreted" by the heart, accounted for people of a *sanguine* temperament; phlegm, secreted by the brain, for a *phlegmatic* temperament; yellow bile, secreted by the liver, for *choleric* temperament; and black bile, secreted by the spleen, *melancholic* temperament.

Four Conditional Temperament Types

We restrict ourselves to a brief description of the four conditional aforementioned types. People of sanguine temperament have a strong nervous system. They are steady in their feelings and actions; they are sociable, talkative, easily conversant with new people. They are very much people persons. They easily adapt to changing life circumstances and are usually hardworking, proactive, confident, inclined to lead. They are effective and creative. The tasks that require frequent switching of attention would be good for people of sanguine temperament. However, representatives of this type may show a tendency "to slide on the surface" and make hasty decisions. They are not very good in performing monotonous work.

Choleric individuals have a strong nervous system, are quick-tempered, straightforward, and aggressive. They are characterized by stable aspirations and persistence in achieving their goals, and they are capable of overcoming great difficulties. They are ambitious, energetic, and passionate and are able to excite people with their cause. They have some difficulties, however, in switching their attention and are not good in performing monotonous work. People of a choleric type of temperament are characterized by the prevalence of excitation over inhibition. They are the ones with "bad brakes," so to say. To put such individuals on the front line of communication with customers, where "customers are always right," is hardly a good idea.

Phlegmatic types are individuals with a strong nervous system. They are balanced, diligent, patient, and peaceful; they tend to be self-content and kind, relaxed and rational. They are not very emotional and not very communicative. They are slow in building skills and habits, but they are persistent toward intended goals. They can work long hours and have a high capacity for work. People of phlegmatic type prefer stability to uncertainty and change. They feel "in their shoes" when the work is laborious and requires patience.

People of melancholic type are individuals with a weak, easily vulnerable nervous system, who are capable of sustaining only short-term stress. They are characterized by high sensitivity, anxiety, and pessimism, and they are introverted and dreamy. They are in need of the continual support of the people around them. They need periodical encouragement even for their everyday performance. It is recommended to note even insignificant progress in their performance. Melancholic type persons are usually perfectionists, can sustain monotonous work, and are creative in poetry and the arts. People of melancholic disposition are often very considerate, self-reliant, and independent.

Now, having briefly described the four temperament types, we have to pause and make an important point. These four general types of temperament rarely exist in a "pure" form. Indeed, many of us exhibit some mixture of Hippocrates' temperament characteristics; that is, all human beings have some degree of each of these four types within them. This is how it can be explained. In any classification, the type is characterized by the severity and the ratio of its constituent properties or other characteristics. Theoretically, the degree of severity of the properties may vary indefinitely, thereby creating an endless number of possible types. However, in reality there is no need for such theorization, and the type approach can be used for practical purposes. Singling out the most prominent feature of temperament assigns a person to one or another type.

Temperament Types and Activity

Is one temperament type better than another in relation to activity? Each temperament type has its strengths and weaknesses, advantages and disadvantages. For example, people with a sanguine temperament are good performers, but they are not that effective in performing monotonous work or work requiring sustained concentration of attention. People of melancholic temperament type are anxious and suspicious, but their ability to pay close attention to details is quite important in a number of professions. In other words, while one temperament type better relates to some kinds of activity, another type is good for some other kinds of activity. All four types have both good and bad qualities in relation to different kinds of activity. Taking subordinates' temperament types and other personality features into account is helpful for managers in the process of implementing their managerial functions. Assigning tasks to people according to their personality features leads to better performance and higher satisfaction in the workplace.

Temperament characterizes people only in terms of the dynamic of their reaction to the event or stimulus; it does not predetermine their mental ability or social significance (Merlin, 1964). People of any temperament type can be good or bad, energetic or lazy, smart or stupid, and so on, in the common sense of the words. A number of famous people were of different temperament types. For example, Russian Tsar Peter the Great and the well-known Russian physiologist Ivan Pavlov belonged to the choleric type of temperament; first Emperor of France Napoleon Bonaparte, one of the greatest military leaders in the history of the West, was sanguine; Field Marshal of the Russian Empire Kutuzov, military commander and diplomat, most widely known for brilliantly repelling Napoleon's invasion of Russia in 1812 was phlegmatic; the great Russian composer Pyotr Ilyich Tchaikovsky and writer Nikolai Gogol, author of the immortal satirical play *Revizor*, both belonged to the melancholic type of temperament. All of them were outstanding people and played a significant role in the life of humankind.

Temperament and the Features of the Nervous System

The Features of the Nervous System

Russian physiologist Ivan Pavlov was the first to establish the link between temperament and the features of the nervous system (Pavlov, 1927). He believed that the properties of temperament are based on the properties of the nervous system. In his experiments on dogs, he discovered three features of the nervous system—*strength*, *mobility*, and *balance*. The latter is the balance of the nervous processes of *excitation* and *inhibition*. Based on various combinations of these three features, he identified four types of the nervous system in relation to Hippocrates' types of temperament: strong, balanced, inert (phlegmatic); strong, balanced, mobile (sanguine); strong, unbalanced, mobile (choleric); weak, unbalanced, mobile or inert (melancholic). Despite the fact that the discovery was based on his experiments on dogs (Pavlov, 1951), Pavlov clearly pointed out that there is every reason to transfer the dogs' types of the nervous system to humans. However, at the same time, he emphasized that humans significantly differ from animals due to the existence of the so-called "second signal systems".[1]

There are two signal systems. The first signal system is the system of conditional reflexes, which is a direct reflection of reality from the external and internal environments in the form of feelings and perceptions via the nerve receptors; that is, the animal brain reacts only to visual, acoustic, and other stimuli. This signal system is common to humans and animals. The second signal system (thinking, consciousness, speech) is inherent only to people. Humans developed this new specifically human form of reflection—the system of audio and visual words. This is a fundamental difference in brain function between animals and people. People possess an ability to think abstractly, allowing for the generalizing of the countless signals from the outer and inner worlds with words. Pavlov called the second signal system "the signals of signals." One more point, Pavlov pointed out that, depending on the predominance of one or the other signal system people belong to, people are either artistic or thinking or medium types.

A strong nervous system manifests itself in greater endurance and in the ability to perform activities in stressful situations. The opposite pole of strength is a weak nervous system, which correlates with poor endurance, a limited ability in resisting stress, and so on. It should be noted that sometimes highly motivated individuals with a weaker nervous system can perform as effectively as the ones with a strong nervous system, or even better. However, such highly motivated behavior of the latter results in exhaustion and fatigue much sooner and may negatively influence their health condition. Pavlov believed that representatives of the weak type of the nervous system are socially inferior. In later years, Soviet psychologists Teplov (1961) and Nebylitsin (1965), by focusing their research on the properties of the nervous system rather than on the types, proposed and proved the hypothesis that the strength of the nervous system is inversely proportional to the sensitivity of the nervous system. The concluding outcome of their studies was, "The nervous system gains from strength but loses in sensitivity" (Teplov, 1985). Thus, the weakness of the nervous system has been "acquitted" and has not been treated as a negative feature of the nervous system anymore. The sensitivity we are talking about is the sensitivity of the so-called "analyzers".[2]

The Analyzers

Each analyzer consists of three interconnected components: peripheral, conductor, and central. Receptors serve as the peripheral links of analyzers; they are the nerve endings or specialized nerve cells that respond to changes in the environment. Some receptors are relatively simple (nerve endings); others are more complex (elements of sensory organs, for example, the retina of the eye). The conductors are the centripetal neurons; they serve as pathways from receptors to the cortex. The core component of the analyzers is the central part where analysis of the information delivered to the brain in a form of nerve impulses from the relevant receptor takes place. All components of the analyzer are an integral whole. Violation of one of them causes the disturbance or malfunctioning of the analyzer as a whole. For example, if the optic nerve is damaged, but an eye and the core component are not, the information perceived by the peripheral component will not be able to travel to the cortex for the analysis. We can say that the person will be able to look but will not be able to see. The biological role of the analyzers is to ensure the appropriate responses to the changing conditions that contribute the most in the process of adaptation to the surrounding world and to preserving the relative constancy of the body's internal environment.

Generally speaking, sensitivity has an adaptive meaning to living beings in their environment; they are more perceptive of the surroundings and react more keenly to it. The famous expression "survival of the fittest" should be understood in Darwin's own metaphor as the "better adapted for the immediate, local environment" but not in the common inference "in the best physical shape." This explains the fact of the existence of the weak types. Animals with a weak nervous system have an advantage of higher sensitivity; they have a better chance of detecting danger early, discover food, and so on. If they did not have such an advantage, they would have long been extinguished by natural selection.

The mobility of the nervous system has to do with the "speed of reconditioning" in the changing external environment. The ability of an individual to demonstrate frequent changes of actions and reactions indicates high mobility. For example, the ability to switch attention quickly is a sign of high mobility. The opposite of mobility is inertness, that is, reduced mobility. However, just as the weakness of the nervous system is not a negative quality, inertness is not a negative quality either. Inert people can perform mobile activity as effectively as individuals with the mobile nervous system by unconsciously compensating their inertness with some prophylactic actions. In spite of their visible slowness, they can effectively perform the activity that requires frequent switching of attention. Klimov (1969) in his studies identified that they were able to achieve such performance by prophylactic measures and by a detailed approach to given tasks in advance.

The third important feature of the nervous system is the balance of the nervous processes of excitation and inhibition, the dynamic quality. It determines how quickly and easily excitatory or inhibitory reflexes may be shaped. The nervous system that leads to the repeated formation of positive associations is considered dynamic in relation to excitation. The nervous system that provides the quick formation of inhibitory reflexes is considered dynamic in relation to inhibition. Dynamic qualities provide not only the rapid formation of elementary reflexes but the formation of more complicated connections as well. This feature of the nervous system correlates with the ability to learn.

The features of temperament depend upon the structural relationships among the diverse features of the nervous system; that is, an individual may possess both strong excitatory and strong inhibitory processes. When strong excitatory processes dominate strong inhibitory processes, it indicates unbalance. When weak excitatory processes dominate weak inhibitory processes, it also indicates unbalance. However, in the case of the former, the person may demonstrate unrestrained passion, which is the characteristic of choleric type of temperament, whereas in the latter case the person may exhibit an agitation and impulsiveness with hysterical quality, which is the characteristic of melancholic type of temperament. It's important to note that after Pavlov's death, his teaching about "four types" came to be regarded as the essence of his theory of types of the nervous system, which overshadowed a truly great discovery by Pavlov—the discovery of the properties of the nervous system.

Extraversion—Introversion and Neuroticism—Stability

> How to differentiate introvert from extravert in a bar? After consuming a fair amount of alcohol, the introvert talks about himself, whereas the extravert talks about others.
>
> A joke

When asked to describe a person, we usually point out the typical way the person behaves in addition to her other characteristics. For example, we say aggressive or shy, funny or uptight, punctual or tardy, and the like. All the adjectives we use in the description psychologists call "traits." The list of traits can be very long, creating a certain inconvenience for practical use. Psychologists tried to reduce the number of traits and came down to the so-called "Big Five personality traits": neuroticism, extraversion, openness, agreeableness, and conscientiousness. Best known for his study of personality, Hans Eysenck (1970) reduced the number of traits to two. He viewed individual differences as a result of two independent variables: neuroticism–stability and extraversion–introversion. Neuroticism (weak emotions, unstable) and stability (strong emotions) are two poles of the same feature. So are extraversion (outgoing) and introversion (opposite to extraversion) two poles of the same feature.

Eysenck proposed a two-dimensional model of temperament that to him constitutes the temperamental types. He based it on Pavlov's idea regarding the relationship between excitation and inhibition processes and concentrated on the interrelationship between the properties of the nervous system and temperament. By pairing different combinations of neuroticism–stability and extraversion–introversion, Eysenck noted their close similarity to the four ancient temperament types. By Eysenck, high neuroticism in combination with high extraversion is equivalent to the choleric type; high neuroticism in combination with low extraversion is equal to the melancholic type; low neuroticism in combination with high extraversion is equal to the sanguine type; low neuroticism in combination with low extraversion is equal to the phlegmatic type.

Extraversion is a characteristic of people as outgoing. Extraverts are in a constant need of "psychological food" from the social environment; they are excitement seekers. They are characterized by high motor and speech activity. They easily respond to a variety of proposals and get actively involved in their implementation, but, on the other hand, they can easily lose interest and switch to a new activity. Introversion is understandably opposite to extraversion. Introverts are thoughtful, rational, inclined to planning their activity; they are inclined to self-analysis, and they look "inside themselves." Generally speaking, extraversion–introversion has a weaker effect on behavior, while neuroticism–stability has a stronger effect. For example, an introverted manager can learn to behave in an extraverted manner if circumstances require.

Neuroticism can be described as an enduring tendency to experience negative emotional states, such as anxiety, guilt, and depression. They draw some negative scenarios in their mind; their body language reflects their emotional state, and their physiological reactions—blood pressure, pulse count, and the like—evidence the same. Those that score high on neuroticism tend to respond poorly to stress. McCrae and Costa (1986) pointed out a very important difference in coping with stress by people with high and low scores of neuroticism. In their research, they found that people with high scores on neuroticism are "emotion-focused" on stress, and they interpret situations as threatening or hopelessly difficult, while people with low scores in neuroticism (stable) are "problem-focused" and tend to ignore the source of stress. Low indicators on the scale neuroticism–stability reflect emotional stability.

Observations and studies of athletes with high scores on neuroticism showed that they successfully acquire the necessary skills in the training environment, sometimes even faster than the ones with lower scores on neuroticism. However, things often change in the conditions of competition. Athletic competitions demand extremely stringent sustainability of the emotional sphere. The higher the competition level, the stronger are the interfering factors that increase the emotional tension. The author of this book (Voskoboynikov, 1974) in the studies of emotional stability of elite level gymnasts determined a correlation between the degree of neuroticism–stability and success in performance in gymnastics competitions. Gymnasts with lower scores on neuroticism (stable) performed their skills in the stressful competitive environment comparably to their performance in the training environment, sometimes even better. That is, the stimuli of the competitive environment influence their emotional state in a positive way. Gymnasts with higher scores on neuroticism (unstable), particularly in combination with introversion, demonstrated instability in performing their skills in competitions, compared to their performance of the same skills in the training environment. Some of the ways to improve performance stability could be to create training conditions close to the conditions of competition, including different kinds of deliberate interferences and distractions while acquiring the motor skills. With practice, it is possible to learn to minimize the effect of neuroticism to a certain degree.

In identifying personality typology, it's important to consider situational characteristics. To take an approach that extroverts are highly adaptable and emotionally stable, while introverts are inhibited, inert, prone to neuroticism, and unstable, seems overly simplistic and manifests inadequate predictability. In situations with weak stimuli, individuals demonstrating behavior with less emotional stability and greater introversion could be more appropriate, since individuals of such a personality type exhibit a much needed psychological sensitivity in such cases. Emotionally stable extraverts in such situations may even exhibit anger because they are not able to sense weak but significant signals and thus may not understand the reasons for the inconsistencies of their circumstances. However, extraverts are undoubtedly more adaptable to a "strong" environment (stressful conditions), in which introverts may easily fall into depression caused by the nervous exhaustion.

Let's Characterize Character

> Ability can take you to the top, but it takes character to keep you there.
> *John Wooden, NCAA coach (as cited in Ziglar, 2004)*

What Characterizes Character?

The word "character" derives from the Greek *charakter*, meaning "enduring or indelible mark." The Greek philosopher Heraclitus proclaimed that "character is destiny." Not accidentally, a Russian saying goes, "Plant a character, harvest destiny." Character is an aggregate of the most stable psychic traits of personality that manifest themselves in a person's typical style and manner of relationship, in behavior and reactions in various situations, and in diverse kinds of activity. It is, so to say, an imprint of personality. Every feature of character is a feature of personality, but not every feature of personality is a feature of character. Only those features of personality that are clearly expressed and demonstrate themselves systematically in diverse situations are considered features of character. A polite person can occasionally act rudely, but we will not characterize him as rude based on such an action that is nontypical for him. We would most likely say it is totally out of his character. Only if a person systematically behaves in an impolite manner can we characterize him as rude.

Character has a certain plasticity that is important for the process of upbringing. The character of a person develops in activity, first in the family environment, then in the process of studying and later in the work environment. We can observe the manifestation of features of character by the way a person strives to reach her goals. If a person is persistent in spite of the obstacles, we talk about a strong character; if a person does not demonstrate consistency in reaching her goals and gives up easily, we talk about a weak character. Managers can learn a lot from athletes about building character. Athletes do not stop training after a failed competition; they train even harder to achieve better results in the next one. The development of such a quality is imperative for managers in their work with people.

In his book *The Only Way to Win*, Jim Loehr[3] writes:

> Sport is a living lab for witnessing the role that character plays in achievement, personal fulfillment and life satisfaction. The impact of big egos, hubris, selfishness, disrespect, distrust, dishonesty and disloyalty is especially visible. Precisely because the pressures are heightened, the payoffs so visible, and the consequences for failure so clear, the study of sport morality can be especially meaningful to business leaders who want both to access and build character strengths in themselves and in their people.
>
> It is also important to note that many of today's most visible corporate leaders credit their past sport experience for helping them absorb and navigate the pressures of corporate life. It's not uncommon, in fact, for companies to actively seek new hires who have been successful athletes.

The Traits of Character

Character traits can be divided into several basic groups (Platonov, 1982). The first group contains general traits of character, such as honesty, fortitude, conformity, and deliberateness. The second group consists of relationship traits such as friendliness, empathy, civility, or hostility. The third group is made up of work orientations such as attitudes to work requirements, initiative, persistence, ambition or lassitude, task anxiety, passivity, and the like. The fourth group consists of how people relate to themselves: dignity, modesty, pride, narcissism, and so on. In professional activity, a person's character manifests itself in relation to work, to colleagues, to bosses, and to subordinates.

Two individuals with similar or even with practically the same innate biological features, as it is with monozygotic twins, may develop different features of character. Sometimes one of the twins can take the initiative and help the other one. Later on, the other twin may ask for some help in the future. Thus the development of some dependence of the second one on the first one can be observed. Such situations become secured in their minds as conditional reflexes, especially if they were accompanied by deep emotions, and become features of their character. Life circumstances and some other factors may lead to "changes" in a person's character. Many probably have observed these kinds of changes in people's behavior and demeanor due to changes in their social status or position in the society or of an improved financial situation, or some other major change. For example, yesterday's colleague, a great guy, became your boss, and suddenly you discover a "different person" in him. However, that is not due to changes in the person's character; this is rather a manifestation of the existing concealed personality features that opened up as a result of a life change or the like. So it does not change who they are; it rather reveals who they are. Abraham Lincoln quoted: "Nearly all men can stand adversity, but if you want to test a man's character, give him power."

"Inconvenient" Characters

Quite often in life we cannot choose with whom we have to work "in harness"; such individuals are either above us by their position in the hierarchy or are on our team. How to deal with those who have a difficult character? First, it's worth noting that there are variations of how the bad characters manifest themselves. A classic example of that could be when two people have nothing in common, for example, enthusiastic dreamer and hard pragmatist, slack sybarite and industrious businessperson, a strict moralist and flippant bacchanal. It seems self-evident that, with such different views on life, successful cooperation can hardly be possible. However, let's look at the situation from a different angle. Is it always a disadvantage to have different points of view? The difficulty mainly is in recognizing the right of the other opinion to exist. That's why, if your destiny puts you in such a conflict situation, the smartest thing would be not to succumb to the first negative impression. Try to understand the other person's preferred way of dealing, performing, and operating; it will help to prevent possible interpersonal conflicts. Try to admit to yourself that the person is annoying not because she is a bad person but because she is different—she is not like you. By the way, she probably has the same problem with you as you have in relation to her. Try to find something positive in that person. It may be easier than it seems. Maybe she is able to resolve difficult tasks better than you are. Do not be afraid to make a first step on the road to mutual understanding. Most likely she will accept your dedication and will take the step toward you. As long as you are "pulling the same wagon" with the person, the first desirable thing to do would be to clearly identify each other's responsibilities and then try not to interfere in the person's "zone of responsibility." If there is a need to ask for an explanation, do it in a neutral tone of voice. Accordingly, answers to the questions should be in a polite manner, even if you think they are irrelevant. It is better than damaging the relationship and then trying to reestablish it. Generally speaking, recognizing a problem on time and not letting it get blown out of proportion may be the way to create reasonably acceptable relationships.

When facing people with bad characters, the main thing to do is to keep calm. Try to avoid negative reactions; otherwise, it will make it more difficult to find common language in the future. Try to put yourself in the other person's shoes; it will help you to better understand the reason he behaves that way. Always try to see further than what it seems like on the surface. Calculate your reaction before acting on it. And it is always better to attack the problem than a person.

In summary, character is the distinctive feature of personality that makes you who you are. In character, such personality features as disposition, charm, spirit, and integrity manifest themselves in relations with other people.

Chapter 2 in a Few Lines

1. People perceive the world through their unique individuality. Always remember that in front of you is not some abstract creature but a living person, most likely different from you.
2. In the most general terms, every human being is characterized by two components: biological and social. Each component is responsible for human development.
3. Sanguine, choleric, phlegmatic, and melancholic are the most common types of temperament. Life demands are so broad that in some circumstances one temperament type is good, and another temperament type is good in different circumstances.
4. Temperament characterizes only the dynamic of behavior and does not define the social significance of the individual.
5. Different combinations of neuroticism/stability and extraversion/introversion have a close similarity to the four ancient temperament types.
6. Extraversion is an outgoing characteristic of people; extraverts are in a constant need of "psychological food" from the social environment, and they are characterized by high motor and speech activity. Introversion is the opposite of extraversion; introverts are thoughtful, rational, inclined to self-analysis.
7. Neuroticism can be described as an enduring tendency to experience negative emotional states. People with high scores on neuroticism are emotion-focused on stress; people with low scores in neuroticism (stable) are problem-focused.
8. There are two signal systems. The first signal system is the system of conditional reflexes, which is a direct reflection of reality from the external and internal environments in the form of feelings and perceptions via the nerve receptors. This signal system is common for humans and animals. The second signal system (thinking, consciousness, speech) is inherent only to people.
9. Character is an aggregate of the most stable psychic traits of personality, which manifest themselves in a person's typical style and manner of behavior.

Notes

1 Pavlov introduced the term "signal systems" in 1932 while studying the physiological mechanism of speech.
2 Pavlov introduced the definition of analyzer in 1909.
3 Jim Loehr has spent over 20 years coaching Fortune 500 executives, world-class athletes, and other high achievers. He describes his methods in the book *The Only Way to Win: How Building Character Drives Higher Achievement and Greater Fulfillment in Business and Life*.

References

Bedny, G. Z. and Karwowski, W. (2007). *Systemic-Structural Theory of Activity: Applications to Human Performance and Work Design*. Boca Raton, FL: Taylor & Francis, CRC Press.
Bedny, G. Z., Karwowski, W. and Voskoboynikov, F. (2010). The relationship between external and internal aspects in activity theory and its importance in the study of human work. In G. Z. Bedny and W. Karwowski (Eds.). *Human–Computer Interaction and Operators' Performance: Optimizing Work Design with Activity Theory*, 31–62. Boca Raton, FL: Taylor & Francis, CRC Press.
Eysenck, H. J. (1970). *The Structure of Human Personality*. London: Methuen.
Gardner, H. (1985). *The Mind's New Science: A History of the Cognitive Revolution*. New York: Basic Books.
Karwowski, W., Voskoboynikov, F. and Bedny, G. Z. (2012). On the relationship between external and internal components of activity. In K. Stanney and K. S. Hale (Eds.). *Advances in Cognitive Engineering and Neuroergonomics*, 109–115. Boca Raton, FL: Taylor & Francis, CRC Press.
Klimov, E. A. (1969). *Individual Style of Activity*. Kazan: Kazan University Press.
Loehr, J. (2012). *The Only Way to Win: How Building Character Drives Higher Achievement and Greater Fulfillment in Business and Life*. New York: Hachette Books.
McCrae, R. R. and Costa, P. T. (1986). Personality, coping, and coping effectiveness in an adult sample. *Journal of Personality*, 54, 385–405.
Merlin, V. S. (1964). *Outlines of Theory of Temperament*. Perm, Russia: Perm Pedagogical Institute.

Nebylitsin, V. D. (1965). *Basic Features of Man's Neural System*. Moscow: Education Publishers.
Pavlov, I. P. (1927). *Conditioned Reflex*. London: Oxford University Press.
Pavlov, I. P. (1951). *Complete Collected Works*, Volume 3, Book 2. Moscow: Academy of Science.
Platonov, K. K. (1982). *System of Psychology and Theory of Reflection*. Moscow: Science Publishers.
Rubinshtein, S. L. (1935). *Foundation of Psychology*. Moscow: Pedagogy Publishers.
Rubinshtein, S. L. (1946). *Foundation of General Psychology*. Moscow: Academic Pedagogical Science.
Skinner, B. F. (1974). *About Behaviorism*. New York: Knopf.
Teplov, B. M. (1961). The theory of types of higher nervous activity and psychology. *Problems of Psychology*, 1, 3–16. Moscow: Education Publishers.
Teplov, B. M. (1985). Examination of the features of the neural system as a method of approaching individual psychological differences. In B. M. Teplov (Ed.). *Individual Differences*. Collection of Works, Volume 2, 137–168. Moscow: Pedagogy.
Voskoboynikov, F. A. (1974). An attempt to use Eysenck's personality test for the diagnosis of emotional stability of elite level gymnasts in the conditions of competition. *Theory and Practice of Physical Culture* (All–Soviet Union monthly journal), 8, 32–33. Moscow.
Ziglar, Z. (2004). *Great Quotes from Zig Ziglar: 250 Inspiring Quotes from the Master Motivator and Friends*. New York: Gramercy Books.

3

PERSONALITY FEATURES AND PERFORMANCE

All kinds of human activity require a number of qualities of a person in order to perform. Some personality features better relate to the requirements of activity, others don't. People are able to compensate their weak qualities by the more outstanding ones. That in turn allows people with different qualities to adapt to the requirements of activity and perform equally effectively. It suggests that in the process of management to rely on people's strong qualities is more effective than to insist on fixing the weaker ones. As a result, you as a manager will best benefit from what people are capable of, and they will experience satisfaction by their performance. You may support the person in her attempts to fix the weak qualities, but to keep pointing them out will hardly do any good. Respect people's individuality and use it the best possible way. Eventually, doing so will benefit your team and the organization.

Nature vs. Nurture: Is it Worth Debating?

About the Debate

The *perennial* debate about what is more potent for the development of human personality—nature or nurture—is still going on today. Most modern researchers' positions fall into a fifty-fifty ratio. Some hold the position that genetics is the prevailing factor in forming personality, while others consider social factors as more significant. For example, gene researcher Craig Venter[1] states that environment, not genes, is key to our personality. That is, the degree to which genes influence human development depends on the kind of environment a human is placed in. Matthew Syed (2010) holds the position that "talent is overrated." He practically dismisses the notion of predetermination by means of heredity on performance. He suggests that "ten thousand hours of purposeful practice" enables a person to achieve an outstanding performance level regardless of his heredity. Purposeful practice, by his definition, is the practice with concentration and dedication, and with an access "to the right training system." Syed followed the lives of such outstanding people as Mozart, Picasso, Federer, and others. He asserted that the outstanding performances these individuals demonstrated in early childhood were due to the thousands of hours of practice that they already had by that time. It is well-known that Mozart's outstanding musical talent emerged as early as the age of three. In all fairness, it's hard to imagine how he could have "ten thousand hours of purposeful training" by such an early age. Scientists, who hold the view that abilities are biologically determined and their expression depends entirely on inherited characteristics, argue that upbringing and education can only speed up the development of abilities.

Edison in a famous quote stated, "Genius is one percent inspiration, ninety-nine percent perspiration" (as cited in Rosanoff, 1932). One percent, of course, should be understood in a relative term, but nevertheless this percent is crucially important. If a person does not have that needed percentage, then the hard work may only advance him to a certain level but not likely to an outstanding level of performance. For example, can anyone without the specific innate makings become an outstanding dancer such as Russian dancer Mikhail Baryshnikov? Can a person with the body size of 7 feet and over 300 pounds become an outstanding gymnast? Never mind outstanding—a gymnast at all? Can you imagine this mass rotating on the high bar and doing double and triple somersaults in the air? If one's biological features do not correspondent to the particular activity, the person can progress only to a certain level of performance but hardly to the outstanding level. In other words, is hard work enough to succeed in a chosen activity? We can work as hard as we want, but if we create blunders along the way, we are just not good at what we do. Nothing can take the place of talent in a chosen activity. Buckingham and Clifton, the authors of *Now, Discover Your Strengths* (2001), maintain that "practice does not necessarily make perfect; to develop strength in any activity requires certain natural talent. You will only excel by maximizing your strengths, never by fixing your weaknesses." They understand strength not only as the ability to demonstrate near perfect performance but, most importantly, to demonstrate it consistently. If a person has no voice, will the "ten thousand hours of purposeful training" make her or him a singer? Larry A. Thompson (2004), who has managed the careers of over 200 artists, stated it authoritatively: "The most common mistake people make is concentration on the weak qualities instead of using the strengths. If you have no ear for music, why try to become a singer?"

In these examples, we mentioned people's physical abilities, but the described phenomenon has as much to do, if not more, with the cognitive, mental, and emotional manifestations of personality as well. A person who is afraid of heights is unlikely to become a mountain climber or a worker in skyscraper construction. It is very unlikely that a person with a weak nervous system will be reliable in performing the stressful work of an operator of a modern automatic control system. A hypothetical example: In the event of an accident in a highly automated technological system, an operator managing the complex has to discover the causes of the accident and eliminate it. If, at this critical time, she isn't able to withstand stress and cannot correct the situation, no matter how highly her work is valued in a nonemergency, this situation will reveal her unreliability in that position.

The "Neglected" Element in the Debate

One very important element seems as though it has not been given enough attention to in the nature–nurture debate: namely, the negative impact on human health due to the discrepancies between personality features and the requirements of an activity. If this is the case, it will not only limit a person's performance level but may lead to the undesired consequences in the health condition as a result of the constant resistance to the elevated stress level. Famous Soviet ballet dancer Maya Plisetskaya once responded to the question about the duration of the ballet life: "Basically it depends on the person's individual abilities. There are people who torture their body, they tear it down by the reinforced stretching and by jumping to the exhaustion, and by over bending to all directions; then we see them walking on crutches in their forties" (Sologubova, 2009). Hence, for such people, achieving an outstanding performance would hardly be possible without harming their health. Indeed, is it worth doing if the person does not have what it takes to achieve an outstanding level of performance? Repetitive training without the underlying talent will lead to early burnout. Prolonged resistance to stress factors does not go "unpunished."

Here is a real-world example from Russian psychologist and former military pilot Marischuk (Marischuk, Platonov and Pletnitsky, 1969) of how a mismatch between the psychological and physiological features of personality on the one hand and objective requirements of activity on the other hand impacted negatively on the human health.

> In 1960s, in Leningrad Aviation Academy (now, St. Petersburg Aviation Academy, Russia), they conducted the following experiment. Upon applying to the Academy for study all applicants went through the required physiological and psychological tests. Some of them did not do very well, but demonstrated strong desire to become pilots. Exceptions were made for those applicants and they were accepted. Within first and second years of study and training some of that particular group dropped out because they could not keep up with the requirements of the training program. The remaining part of the group continued their study and training demonstrating strong will in mastering the profession despite their inadequate to the activity physiological and psychological properties. They completed the full program and graduated as pilots. However, in a few years all of them were discharged from the service due to the different chronic health disorders as a result of the highly stressful for them activity.

Prolonged resistance to the impact of the excessive objective requirements of an activity creates a state of stress that makes the body more vulnerable to diseases and eventually leads to the breakdown of the weakest link in the organism. That's exactly what happened to those pilots. Some of them developed disorders of the gastrointestinal tract, others high blood pressure and disorders of a similar nature. Indeed, the chain is only as strong as its weakest link.

The most famous scientist in stress research, Hans Selye, once wrote of the rabbit and the turtle. Some of us approach life more like a rabbit, running from place to place, nibbling when we can, shooting off in all directions. Others approach life more like a turtle, proceeding methodically from point to point with careful attention to detail, taking things one at a time. Both extremes are healthy. What is unhealthy, or stressful, is trying to be different from our nature. For example, the rabbit says to her turtle spouse, "You never want to go anywhere or to do anything." The turtle, feeling guilty, decides to become a rabbit for the night and go barhopping with the rabbit spouse. That, Selye says, is what causes stress—being untrue to our nature (cited in Howard, 1994).

The Twin Study Method on the Debate

The significance of the role that genetics plays in the developing of personality has been observed in twin studies. Monozygotic (identical) twins are developed from a single egg; they have identical genetic coding. Dizygotic (fraternal) twins are developed from two different eggs. The scientific study of human twins began back in the 1870s by Charles Darwin's cousin, Sir Francis Galton. He was the one who coined the nature–nurture controversy phrase. He published a series of articles in which he argued that heredity (nature) is stronger than environment (nurture) in determining the respective characteristics of twins. Modern researchers using the twin method more accurately assess the role of heredity and environment in the development of skills. The studies have compared the performance abilities of monozygotic twins and just brothers and sisters. It was found that the ability and level of development within the monozygotic pairs coincide in 70–80% of cases and 40–50% in pairs of siblings. These studies have confirmed that abilities, or at least the makings, are most closely related to heredity. A comparative study of monozygotic twins who were brought up in different families shows that their individual psychological and behavioral manifestations are very similar to those of twins who grew up in the same family.

What is important for our consideration is that the biological components of personality significantly predetermine the ability to perform. The plasticity of human innate peculiarities is not unlimited. The limitations take effect when innate individual features of personality are not up to the objective requirements of an activity. In such cases, the only way to connect the activity to the individuals is by professional selection.

The role of genetics does not in any way diminish the social role in human development. Representatives of this point of view believe that the psyche features are entirely determined by the quality of education and training. The development of abilities is largely determined by the role of environment in which the person lives and acts, but proponents of this theory go further. They refer to cases where children of the most backward and primitive tribes, having received appropriate training, were no different from educated Europeans. As a part of this approach, they talk about social exclusion and a shortage of communication as the reasons these tribes remained at a primitive level of development, not because of their innate abilities or makings. These cases are evidence of another important factor in the debate, namely, the impossibility of human development outside human society. Despite all the debate, the essential question remains unanswered: Which is more important for the development of abilities—heredity or environment. But, then again, is the question worth debating?

The Rationale

Where does the nature–nurture debate stand now? Proponents of each side continue to present facts from their studies. Both nature and nurture play important roles in human development. The most rational statement on the subject of the nature–nurture debate, in our opinion, has been articulated by Warren Bennis (2003):

> There are people who claim that our destiny resides wholly in our genes, that each of us is a mere product of heredity. Others argue fervently that each of us is an offspring of his or her environment, and that our life is determined by our circumstances. Studies of identical twins that have been raised separately indicate that there is more truth to the first perspective. But the real answer to how we become who we are is more complex. Recent genetic research affirms that there is a strong hereditary component to disease. Nevertheless, equally compelling research suggests that whether we succumb to various disorders can be ascribed to such environmental factors as stress. In the great debate between hereditary determinism and environmental determinism, there is not much room left for self-determination. In a sense, both schools justify removing responsibility for behavior from the individual. The truth is we are products of everything—genes, environment, faith, friends, trade winds, earthquakes, sunspots, schools, accidents, serendipity, anything you can think of, and more. The endless nature–nurture debate is interesting, even occasionally revelatory, but inconclusive. And it's about as useful as a guide to life as an astrological chart.

Goleman (2006) formulated the rationale on the debate in a shorter version: "The debate turns out to be pointless based on the fallacy that our genes and our environment are independent of each other; it's like arguing over which contributes more to the area of a rectangle, the length or the width."

Human Abilities and Activity

The Makings—The Base of Abilities

Why do people who find themselves in identical or nearly identical conditions achieve different levels of performance? Why do we observe rapid assimilation of knowledge or acquisition of skills among some people but a long and painful learning process among others? To answer these questions, we will appeal to the notion of abilities. However, before talking about abilities, let's briefly consider the base for abilities—the makings. The makings are the anatomical and physiological features of the nervous system that constitute a natural basis of abilities. Structural features of the central nervous system are innate features; they are only the makings of abilities, that is, the prerequisites for the development of abilities and not the abilities themselves.

The individual features of different analyzers (mentioned in the previous chapter) are a natural basis of abilities. For example, certain characteristics of auditory perception can serve as a basis for the development of musical abilities. Thus, abilities should be understood as the individual characteristics that are the basis for the successful implementation of one or many kinds of activity. Abilities determine the dynamic of acquiring knowledge and skills, the capacity to process information as well as the overall level of accomplishments. Abilities, just like other features of personality, are formed and demonstrated through activity, they provide rapid acquisition, consolidation, and the effectiveness of their application to practice.

The presence of the makings does not necessarily mean that a person will develop certain skills. Returning to the previous example, an essential prerequisite for the development of musical abilities is a subtle ear, but the structure of the peripheral (ear) and central nervous system is only a prerequisite to the development of musical abilities. To what extent the makings will be developed into musical abilities depends on the conditions of the individual's life circumstances. Thus, the development of innate individual features is a socially conditioned process that is associated with upbringing and education and with the development of the society. Even though abilities are not to be reduced to knowledge and skills, it must be noted that abilities cannot exist disconnected from knowledge and skills. If a person ceases to practice, abilities will not continue to develop and will be lost with time. Only by systematic practice will abilities further develop.

General and Special Abilities

Specific human abilities are divided into general and special higher intellectual abilities. They can be divided into theoretical and practical, educational and creative, substantive and interpersonal, and so on. General abilities include the ones that define success in a variety of human activities. For example, intellectual ability, memory, speech, subtle hand movements, and others are included in the category of general abilities. Those are the abilities inherent to most people. Special abilities refer to those that determine success in specific human activities, such as musical, mathematical, linguistic, technical, literary, artistic, athletic, and the like. The presence of common abilities does not preclude the development of special abilities and vice versa. The abilities that manifest themselves in communication and interaction with people are also included in general human abilities. These abilities are socially conditioned and are formed in humans in the process of socialization. Without the assimilation of speech as a means of communication, without the ability to adapt to human society, without the ability to perceive and evaluate the actions of others and build relations in various social situations, a normal life and human mental development would simply be impossible.

The high level of special abilities is talent (music, literature, science, athleticism, etc.). The word "talent" is found in the Bible, as the measure of the value of silver, which slaves received from their master. Originally the word "talent" was known in ancient Greece, Babylon, and Persia as the biggest weight and monetary unit. If a slave who received the money preferred to bury it in the ground instead of putting it into circulation and make a profit, people refer to that as "burying the talent in the ground." In modern language, this term has acquired the figurative connotation due to its new meaning, and it is used when a person does not care about the development of his abilities. In addition to other abilities, talent shows and develops only in activity and is influenced by the development of society.

The highest degree of ability is called "genius." Geniuses are those who by their creative achievements have a profound and lasting effect on society and culture. People of genius are very few in number. Among those who have achieved such universalism and could be called geniuses are Aristotle, Leonardo da Vinci, Descartes, Einstein, and a few others. Geniuses are people with an absolute obsession and desire for limitless perfection. The study of the biographies of the geniuses of all time leads to the inevitable conclusion that geniuses are born. But the greatest talents, even with the internal impulse, do not guarantee perfection. The vast majority of potential geniuses' gift of nature is extinguished by inadequate upbringing, by insufficient incentives, and other influences. Only a small part of potential geniuses are developed into real geniuses.

Abilities and Skills and Knowledge and Intelligence

Abilities and skills are often confused, leading to erroneous conclusions. The following is a real-world classic example of such a misinterpretation of abilities. The famous Russian artist of the 19th century Vasily Surikov once made an unsuccessful attempt to enter the St. Petersburg Academy of Fine Arts. Although his outstanding abilities were detected early enough, he lacked the necessary skills in drawing. The Academy's committee denied his admission. The committee's mistake was that they were unable to distinguish between Surikov's abilities and his lack of drawing skills. Within the following three months, Surikov mastered the required skills, and the same committee found him worthy of admission to the Academy.

Similarly, the misinterpretation of abilities of other outstanding people has its place in history. Albert Einstein was an average student at school. In his high school graduation certificate, there are only six excellent marks out of 14 subjects; in other subjects, his marks were good and average. In fact, Einstein failed the entrance exams to the prestigious Polytechnic Institute in Zurich, Switzerland, on his first try. Then he spent a year studying at a local high school, retook the entrance exam, and passed it. Russian writer Nikolai Gogol, author of the immortal comedy *Revizor*, did not know how to write essays and often received Ds. In a Russian literature class, teachers scored him with no more than C. Soviet poet and essayist Osip Mandelshtam, a genius, was called "a walking encyclopedia" (Kuzina, 2008). His contemporaries used to say, wake him up in the middle of the night, ask any question, and you will receive a comprehensive response. But, whether due to some distraction or his persistent rejection of pressure of any kind, he failed one test after another.

The same way as abilities and skills are sometimes confused, knowledge and intelligence are often confused too. Hardly anyone objects to the notion that knowledge is power; however, knowledge obtained by studying does not necessarily constitute one's intelligence. Some people are successful in studying and in passing tests and exams, others are not, but it does not mean that they are not intelligent in their own practical way. Intelligence (from the Latin *intellectus*) is recognized as every person's inherent ability to use mental operations, which is one of the fundamental characteristics of intelligence. Compared to an average person, creative people project a divergent thinking and usually search for solutions in a wide spectrum that allow them to find highly unusual decisions. Academic abilities determine the success of learning and assimilating knowledge and skills, whereas creative abilities, as a manifestation of intelligence, determine the possibility of discoveries and inventions.

In the 1990s, a group of academic researchers issued a scientific statement on intelligence (Gottfredson, 1997). Here is one of their conclusions:

> Intelligence is a very general mental capability that, among others, involves the ability to reason, plan, solve problems, think abstractly, comprehend complex ideas, learn quickly and learn from experience. It is not merely book learning, a narrow academic skill, or test taking smarts. Rather it reflects a broader and deeper capability for comprehending our surroundings—"catching on", "making sense" of things, or "figuring out" what to do.

From the perspective of human development, both knowledge and intelligence in humans are important. On the one hand, if humanity were deprived of the opportunity to create, it would likely have not developed. But, on the other hand, if people did not have the academic skills—the learning ability—the development of humanity would, again, be impossible. Thus, both the ability of people to absorb the knowledge accumulated by previous generations and creative ability make up the way for humanity to advance.

The IQ Question and "Bad Student" Phenomenon

> Good students become good doctors; bad students become chief doctors.
> Russian ironic proverb

This ironic proverb reflects the system of moving up the hierarchical ladder in the former Soviet Union during the time of "socialist realism." Of course, such a phenomenon took place not only in the medical field but everywhere in the country. Quite often those whose professional skills were not good enough for working as "ordinary" specialists occupied leading positions in industries and fields because of their Communist Party membership. In the Soviet Union, it was a very well-known prerequisite for a career advancement. Quite commonly, a former "bad student" Communist Party member held a position of the director of a plant, whereas a former "good student" non–Communist Party member was the chief engineer. Someone had to "turn the wheels." The privileges that members of the Communist Party possessed in the former Soviet Union is a whole other matter that is not the subject of this book. Instead we will attempt to analyze the "bad student" phenomenon from the psychology of management point of view. It will allow us to see the phenomenon from a very different angle.

Back in 1912, German psychologist William Stern proposed to measure intellectual ability using the now known factor of IQ (intellectual quotient). Since then, for decades businesspeople and professionals have paid much attention to IQ for the purpose of placing workers based on their best abilities, as they thought this was the best approach. However, as it happens sometimes, a good idea can be taken too far. This seems to be the case with the notion of IQ. Tests are designed for identifying not talent but rather skills and knowledge. Tests are used not for identifying natural (innate) differences between people but rather for their preparedness for the test at the time of the test. Test results may be influenced by cultural differences, by past education, even by the stopwatch, among other factors. Test supporters can hardly object to the fact that those who can't pass the test will successfully pass it after some practice. As to good judgment and effective managerial decision making, standardized testing does not predict that. On the same note, education does not predict successful managerial performance either. Intelligence, not education, is the key to successful managerial performance. Albert Einstein once said, "I am enough of the artist to draw freely upon my imagination. Imagination is more important than knowledge. Knowledge is limited. Imagination encircles the world" (1929).

Eighty-six years since the IQ test was introduced, Daniel Goleman in his book *Emotional Intelligence* (1998) explained that control over one's own emotions and the ability to perceive the feelings of others describe intelligence more accurately than the ability to think logically. It means that, for practical application, the EQ (emotional intelligence) is a more important factor than IQ. In other words, it makes emotional intelligence more significant and more important for success in business and life. According to Goleman's research, EQ is crucial for the effectiveness of management: 85% of success is determined by EQ, and only 15% is determined by IQ. In his study, Goleman confirmed that, for managers, the ability to listen and hear others is much more important than just to use their own knowledge. On the same accord, the ability to ask the right questions is much more important than the ability to give direct and clear instructions.

But let's go back to the beginning of the 20th century. After the IQ tests were enthusiastically embraced, Columbia University psychologist Edward Thorndike (1920) defined the ability to understand and manage people as social intelligence. He pointed out that "the best mechanic in the factory may fail as a foreman for the lack of social intelligence." Almost at the same time, in 1926, Ernst Holmes (1991), an American spiritual writer, described the so-called "PQ (personality quotient)". He wrote that PQ is more important than IQ: "[K]een, hard-headed business employers have come to see that a man's I.Q. is not nearly so important as is his P.Q., and this is what they are now insisting upon. Is he the kind of person who makes friends easily, gets along well with the public, as well as with his co-workers? Will he be an asset to the firm?" With that in mind, the researchers at one of the leading universities decided to investigate the relative merits of IQ and PQ. Two groups of university graduates were chosen without their knowing it. One group of 100 brilliant IQ men was listed, and their careers were watched for results. All of them did remarkably well academically but failed to mix with their fellows, probably because of their great interest in studies. They had been the typical introvert type, interested solely in high educational standards. Another group of 100 consisted of graduates whose academic standings had been so mediocre that they had only barely succeeded in passing but whose genial qualities of personality had made them so popular that they were greatly liked by all who knew them. At the end of ten years it was found that those brilliant IQ men were making on the average three times less a year than the PQ men. The PQ men liked people, people liked them and liked to have them around.

But the most interesting study on the subject of personality was conducted by Harvard psychologists during the time of the Great Depression (Holmes, 1991). The psychologists knew that, due to the tough economic times, it would be impossible to keep employed all those available. The object of the study was to determine the real cause for the dismissal from employment of many. It took place in Boston and continued for a period of one year. The study involved 4,000 men. To get a general cross-section of the situation, different classes of workers were chosen for the study: unskilled, skilled, clerical, professional, and executive. And, as it is in most cases of psychological experiments, neither the employers nor the employees were aware of the object of the study. Upon the completion of the study, after all the figures were compiled, the psychologists were startled by the outcome. The majority of the reasons for dismissal were not "poor performance" or "reduction of overhead expenses" or "reduction of volume of work" or similar ones. No, these reasons represented only a small number of those who were fired. Here are the figures of the dismissals by categories: 16% had lost their jobs because of the lack of ability to perform, 8% because of immorality or misdemeanors, 13% because of miscellaneous reasons; 63% (!) had lost their positions simply because they did not get along with their associates. It was an astonishing fact, especially taking into account the crucial job market period of that time.

More recently Claudio Fernández-Aráoz (2007), a top global expert on hiring and promotion decisions, found, in an analysis of new C-level executives, that those who had been hired for their self-discipline, drive, and intellect were later fired for lacking basic social skills. In other words, the people whom Fernández-Aráoz studied had smarts in spades, but their inability to get along socially on the job was professionally self-defeating. Good social personality is of great importance among other personality traits. Those with good personality are always desirable associates; they attract people, thereby bringing opportunities for advancement. Good personality pays!

Professional Suitability and Reliability

In order to perform any professional activity (or any kind of activity for that matter), a person must meet certain objective requirements that vary with profession. It is implied that any normal human being can be trained to learn any professional trade. Among humans' innate qualities is a great plasticity that allows the vast majority of people to master different professions and perform quite successfully. There are many specific skills that can be learned if a person wants or has to. However, the question is not that it can be learned but how much time and effort it will take for those whose innate features are not up to the requirements of the activity. For example, when two people perform the same work equally successfully, we don't know how each of them came up to the required level of knowledge and skills, how much time and effort each of them put into achieving the needed level of performance.

Russian psychologist Gurevich (1970) studied this phenomenon. He writes:

> Even if to suggest that some special training methods could be found, a person with limited innate properties would have to spend unreasonable amounts of time and energy to master a chosen profession, compared to another person whose innate properties better relate to the activity. The

period of active human life that is limited and unproductive, comprised of depressing activity, would not only bring personal unhappiness, but ultimately will negatively affect the society as a whole.

Based on years of research, Gurevich proposed the division of professions into two types. Professions of the first type are the ones that present excessive requirements to some individuals. He called these requirements *noncompensable*. That is, due to the certain incongruity of the innate features of some individuals to the objective requirements of activity, they either cannot master the profession, or, even if they can, it may have a negative impact on their health.

Reliability, in general terms, refers to consistency in performance. In technical systems, a qualitative characteristic of reliability is "the ability of the system to perform its required functions at a given time interval and under the conditions of overloads for which the system is designed" (Bedny, Karwowski and Bedny, 2015). The human error in the failure of the technical system can occur for various reasons. It can take place as a result of an inadequate equipment design in relation to human factors, leading to erroneous human actions. It can also be as an effect of a mismatch between the properties of humans and activity requirements, which also leads to erroneous human actions. For example, effective performance in some dangerous professions implies that the operator must possess a high level of emotional stability. It manifests itself in the ability to demonstrate learned skills under adverse conditions, such as stress, fatigue, danger, time limit, and so on.

All other professions that present *compensable* requirements are the professions of the second type, the mass professions. Most people can master mass professions and perform successfully without harming their health. Playing a major role in the adaptation to the objective requirements of an activity in mass professions is the so-called "individual style of activity". It manifests itself in the specific strategy that people consciously or unconsciously use in order to adapt to the objective requirements of an activity. However, it should be noted that professional suitability manifests itself in the specific professional activity, whereas the same individual style of activity manifests itself in various kinds of activities.

At this juncture, it would be interesting to speculate on how the selection of people for work on the installation of first skyscrapers in New York took place in the 19th century. No particular occupational selection at the beginning of this period was conducted. Instead, there was the, so to say, "natural self-selection" on the basis of, "I am *not* going to climb up there." The nerve-wracking photographs of workers atop the metal girders is probably the best illustration of the excessive (noncompensable) requirements for some people. Check the photos out on the Internet and imagine yourself sitting or standing up there with a 360-degree view of all New York under your feet. Some people feel dizzy just looking at the photographs.

The Individual Style of Activity

The Concept

All kinds of work, learning, and athletic activity are characterized by the interaction of subjective personality features and the objective requirements of an activity. This interaction goes in two directions. The first one is the adaptation of the objective requirements of the activity to the subjective properties of the individual; the second is in the adaptation of the subjective properties of the individual to the requirements of the activity. Hence, there are two ways to ensure the effectiveness of human performance. One is by professional selection, the so-called "screening out" of individuals with specific attributes. The other is individual training methods directed toward the formation of individual strategies of activity based on the personality features of the individual in the process of adaptation to the objective requirements of the activity.

While in the West the selection method was used more intensively, in the former Soviet Union the attention mostly was directed toward the development of methods for individual training. The concept of an individual style of activity was first introduced by the Soviet psychologist Merlin (1986) and his follower Klimov (1969). In subsequent years, other authors also studied the effect of individual personality features on performance (Bedny and Voskoboynikov, 1975). The outcome of these studies conducted by the authors was the establishment of the fact that different individuals can perform with equal efficiency through the use of their own strategies of performance that are more suitable to their personality features. That is, people attempt to compensate for individual weaknesses with their personal strengths in a given task situation. By implementing the individual style of activity on performance, they diminish the impact of their weaker features of personality. Thus, the central notion in the study of the individual style of activity is that it connects the features of personality with mechanisms of self-regulation and strategies of performance.

Self-Regulation as the Basis for Individual Strategy

As mentioned, all kinds of human activity present more than one objective requirement to people in order to perform. It allows different individuals to rely on their personal strengths to compensate for individual weaknesses. Such a strategy occurs at the conscious and unconscious levels and is based on principles of self-regulation. Both levels are tightly interconnected and transform from one to another. The process of self-regulation manifests itself in the formation of desired goals, in developing a program of actions that correspond to these goals, with conditions for achieving the goals and with persons' individual abilities. In other words, people, through trials, errors, and feedback corrections, create strategies of performance suitable to their individuality. For example, people with an inertial nervous system develop a predisposition to organize and plan their work in advance and attempt to utilize a stereotyped method of performance. Thus, individual styles of activity should be considered as strategies of performance deriving from the mechanism of self-regulation that depend on personality features (Bedny and Seglin, 1999; Voskoboynikov, 2014).

Based on individual style, the subject can adapt to the situation more efficiently. It should be distinguished, however, that individual style of activity and methods of performance are not the same. The latter is dependent not upon individual personality features but rather upon organizational factors, imposed supervisory procedures, and the like. Sometimes methods of performance that derive from organizational factors may contradict individual personality features, which is not desirable. In cases of inadequate training that ignores individual features of personality, the subject may acquire methods of performance that contradict his individuality. It may negatively affect the performance level and the job satisfaction.

Empirical facts and theoretical studies show that the adaptive mechanism of personality traits can work up to a certain limit. If the task presented before a group of people gradually becomes more and more complicated, the following picture can be observed. In the early stages of the task performance, almost all participants show approximately the same results. As the task gets more and more complicated, the differences in results will be demonstrated. People who are able to perform the more complicated task will be assigned to the higher professional category. Those whose individual style of activity will not provide adaptation to the objective requirements of activity will remain in the category of lower regulatory requirements.

It is interesting to identify how subjects disintegrate into distinct groups with respect to their ability to acquire skills. Such disintegration takes place as the capacity of some individuals to adjust to the requirements of the activity is reduced due to the increased task complexity. In simple situations, individuals exhibit similar levels of achievement regardless of their individual style of performance. In such situations, it is hard to identify individual differences, but when the task becomes more complicated, the individuals' performance levels begin to vary. The following hypothetical example can serve as an illustration. If two gymnasts of different levels—intermediate and high—compete in performing intermediate-level gymnastics skills, they will be able to show approximately the same results. However, it does not mean that the gymnast of intermediate level will be able to perform high-level skills even by training for years. The convergence of results in performing the intermediate level skills is possible because the personality features of both gymnasts meet the objective (regulatory) requirements for performing that particular task. When they are presented with a more complicated task, personality features of the intermediate-level gymnast may not be up to the particular activity requirements because this gymnast has already exhausted her potential.

The Study

My colleague and I conducted an experiment on the subject (Bedny and Voskoboynikov, 1975). We chose ten elementary school pupils who, according to the program, were supposed to master addition and subtraction of single-digit numbers. Based on their teacher's evaluations of their mathematical ability, they were split into three subgroups: superior (three exceptionally gifted students), average (four students), and poor (three weak performers). The question at issue was how quickly they would perform the repetitive mathematical calculations. For this purpose, we used the simplest tasks presented in a written form—the addition and subtraction of single-digit numbers.

At the beginning of the experiment, the weaker subjects spent up to 40 minutes to complete the task, whereas advanced subjects spent fewer than 4 minutes, and the average level pupils spent about 20 minutes. Based on these first results, we assumed that these differences would be sustained, which could be explained by the significance of their individualities. However, the overall experimental results were contrary to our expectations. In the following days, average and weaker subjects sharply increased their performance speeds. Subjects with advanced ability exhibited a much flatter learning curve, showing only a slight improvement, suggesting that they were near the ceiling at the outset. Average and weaker subjects continued to reduce their task performance time, approaching the superior students' performance.

Next, our task was to explain how, through training, did subjects with such substantial differences in their mental development improve their performance. Our observation demonstrated that subjects with weaker abilities used their fingers, as well as their external speech. It meant that their mental operations depended on the external practical actions. Only after multiple executions of the task did they start to rely exclusively on internal mental operations. Subjects with average ability also had an initial tendency to rely on external practical actions to perform the task. Their calculations were accompanied by whispers that were barely audible; that is, they facilitated slow mental operations with some external actions. Pupils with advanced abilities started their calculation without any relation to external practical actions from the outset.

Taking the results in consideration, we decided to test the strategies of the subjects by increasing the complexity of the task. We asked the subjects to perform the addition and subtraction of two pairs of numbers. If the preliminary result of a first operation was greater than the result of a second operation, the subjects were to subtract the second from the first. If the second was larger than the first, then they were to add them. In order to frustrate rote memory, the same numbers were used in different positions across several versions of the task. The results of this experiment demonstrated that adaptation abilities were more restricted, compared to the first part of the experiment; that is, subjects of weaker and average groups needed some experimenter's assistance during their first few trials of performing the task. Only the advanced subjects were able to perform the task without any assistance immediately. They demonstrated high levels of performance from the start and stabilized their results within 15 trials, completing the entire task in 1 to 1.5 minutes. In the average group, stabilization of performance occurred after 20 trials and was achieved in 4 to 6 minutes. Among the weaker pupils, stabilization was in the range of 8 to 10 minutes after 20 trials, and there was no further improvement. Then we let them all continue up to trial 30, but from trial 24 to trial 30, there was no improvement in all groups. Thus, in performing relatively simple tasks, subjects were able to reduce differences in performance quite noticeably, whereas increased complexity of the task requirements resulted in distinct groups with distinct levels of performance.

In summary, the individual style of activity is the most efficient method of adaptation to the objective requirements of task performance. From the self-regulation activity point of view, individual styles of activity can be considered strategies of performance that derive from the individual features of personality. Individual style of activity can be formed consciously or unconsciously. In most cases, it forms unconsciously and involuntarily. Though the individual style of activity is the most effective method of adaptation to the objective requirements of an activity, it has its limitations. The limitations take effect when individual features of personality are not up to the requirements of activity. In such cases, the only way to connect the activity to the individual is by professional selection. This differentiation in performance described takes place in mass professions, in many manually performed jobs; some people are just average performers, others are virtuosos.

Chapter 3 in a Few Lines

1. The nature–nurture debate is about what is more important in human development. Most modern researchers are in the ratio of fifty-fifty.
2. Both the biological and the social in personality play their roles in human development.
3. The presence of the makings does not guarantee their development into the ability. Abilities are formed and demonstrated through activity.
4. There are two types of professions from the point of view of adaptation to the requirements of an activity. Professions of the first type present noncompensable requirements for some individuals. Professions of the second type present compensable requirements. These are mass professions. Most people can master mass professions and perform successfully without harming their health.
5. Knowledge obtained by studying does not necessarily constitute one's intelligence. Some people are successful in studying and in passing tests and exams; others are not that good at this, but it does not mean that they are not intelligent in their own practical way.

6. Individual style of activity is the most effective method of adaptation to the objective requirements of activity.
7. You will excel only by maximizing your strengths, not by fixing your weaknesses.

Note

1 Craig Venter is an American biotechnologist, biochemist, and geneticist.

References

Bedny, G. Z., Karwowski, W. and Bedny, I. (2015). *Applying Systemic-Structural Activity Theory to Design of Human-Computer Interaction Systems*. Boca Raton, FL: Taylor & Francis.
Bedny, G. Z. and Seglin, M. (1999). Individual style of activity and adaptation to standard performance requirements. *Human Performance*, 12, 59–78.
Bedny, G. Z. and Voskoboynikov, F. A. (1975). Problems of how a person adapts to the objective requirements of activity. In V. G. Aseev (Ed.). *Psychological Problems of Personality*, Volume 2, 18–30. Irkutsk, Russia: Irkutsk University Press.
Bennis, W. (2003). *On Becoming a Leader*. New York: Basic Books.
Buckingham, M. and Clifton, D. O. (2001). *Now, Discover Your Strengths*. New York: The Free Press.
Einstein, A. (1929). What Life Means to Einstein. Interview by G. S. Viereck. *The Saturday Evening Post*.
Fernández-Aráoz, C. (2007). *Great People Decisions: Why They Matter So Much, Why They Are So Hard, and How You Can Master Them*. Hoboken, NJ: John Wiley & Sons.
Goleman, D. (1998). *Emotional Intelligence*. New York: Bantam Dell.
Goleman, D. (2006). *Social Intelligence*. New York: Bantam Dell.
Gottfredson, L. S. (1997). Mainstream science on intelligence: An editorial with 52 signatories, history, and bibliography. *Intelligence*, 24, 13.
Gurevich, K. M. (1970). *Professional Suitability and Basic Features of the Neural System*. Moscow: Pedagogical Academy of Science.

Holmes, E. (1991). *The Basic Ideas of Science of Mind*. Marina del Ray, CA: DeVorss & Company Publisher.
Howard, P. (1994). *The Owner's Manual for the Brain: Everyday Applications from Mind Brain Research*. Austin, TX: Bard Production Books.
Klimov, E. A. (1969). *Individual Style of Activity*. Kazan: Kazan University Press.
Kuzina, S. (February 12, 2008). Why C-Students Become Managers and A-Students Become Subordinates. *Komsomol'skaya Pravda*, Moscow.
Marischuk, V. L., Platonov, K. K. and Pletnitsky, E. N. (1969). *Tensions in Flight*. Moscow: Voenizdat.
Merlin, V. S. (1986). *Outlines of Integral Study of Individuality*. Moscow: Pedagogy.
Rosanoff, M. A. (September, 1932). Edison in His Laboratory. *Harper's Magazine*.
Sologubova, N., author of the video project. (2009). *The Line of Life, Maya Plisetskaya*. Movie Archive, Russia.
Syed, M. (2010). *Bounce: Mozart, Federer, Picasso, Beckham, and the Science of Success*. New York: HarperCollins.
Thompson, L. A. (2004). *Shine: A Powerful Four-Step Plan for Becoming a Star in Anything You Do*. New York: McGraw-Hill.
Thorndike, E. (1920). Intelligence and Its Use. *Harper's Magazine*, 140, 227–235.
Voskoboynikov, F. (2014). The influence of personality features on performance in work, study and athletic activity. In Tadeusz Marek, Waldemar Karwowski, Marek Frankiwicz, Jussi Kantola and Pavel Zgaga (Eds.). *Human Factor of a Global Society: A System of Systems Perspective*, 187–192. Boca Raton, FL: Taylor & Francis Group.

4

WHAT'S GOING ON IN GROUPS?

It has long been observed that people behave differently in a group setting as compared to their behavior in private. An individual in a group appears in a new capacity—as a component of the system "individual–other individuals." A group of people is not the arithmetic sum of individuals, and group psychology is not the arithmetic mean of the sum of individual consciousnesses. Groups have properties of their own; they are different from the properties of the individuals who form the group. Just as two dozen clear fragments of glass stacked one on another provide a rich blue color, or a combination of copper and tin results in an alloy, the resultant color or hardness is neither of the individual components. Similarly, people in the group act and behave in a new capacity. In most cases a group environment has a positive effect on people's behavior and performance.

People Need People

The Importance of Social Environment for Human Development

The life of every human being from birth to death, one way or another, occurs in the social environment in communication with other people. Social interaction is necessary not only for the normal functioning of the organism and the whole person but for ensuring the survival and education of future generations. Through participation throughout life in various groups, so-called "socialization" takes place. Socialization is understood as the process of mastering the individual social experience, the system of social ties and relationships. It is the process of integrating the individual into the social environment and assimilation to its norms and values. The formation of mentality, habits, character, and other personal characteristics occur through participation in groups. Socialization implies active human participation in the development of human relations culture in the formation of certain social norms, roles, and functions, an acquisition of skills necessary for their successful implementation. In other words, socialization refers to the entire multifaceted process of learning the accumulated experience of life in human society and social relations.

In humankind history are known cases when children, due to circumstances, lived with animals for the first years of their lives. Those are the so-called "feral children". A feral child is a human child who has lived away from human contact from a very young age and was brought up by animals or lived in the wild in isolation. These children usually had little or no experience of human care, of social behavior, and, most importantly, of human language. The only evidence that they were biologically humans was their physical characteristics. Such specific human qualities like speech, consciousness, upright walking, and other qualities were absent in them. The best known case of feral children were two girls captured near Calcutta, India in 1920, who had lived with wolves. The girls were named Kamala and Amala and were thought to be aged about eight and two. Amala died the following year, Kamala survived until 1929, by which time she had given up eating carrion and had learned to walk upright and spoke about 50 words.

Humans, as biological beings, can become persons only in the social environment. Just as for a seed to grow into a plant, it must be planted in the soil, a newborn baby, to become a person, must be situated in social "soil." The social environment is where a newborn can acquire the social and historical experience of humankind and internalize social norms.

Social Facilitation

In the mid-1950s, social psychologist Stanley Schachter (1959) conducted an experiment on the so-called "psychology of isolation". The purpose of the experiment was to see how long people would be able to survive without social contacts. Each of five young men was situated in a separate room. The only things in each room were a table, chair, bed, lamp, and a toilet—no books, magazines, TV. Food for them was left at the door without making social contact. Men were paid for their time and could withdraw from the experiment any time. One of them wanted out in . . . 20 minutes. Three out of the remaining four lasted two days. One of them said that the two days were the most difficult of his life; two others said they felt more and more disoriented as the time progressed. Only one of all five was able to stay in isolation for eight days.

In his other experiment, the subjects were divided into two groups. Members of the first group were told that they would be subjected to a relatively strong impact of electric current. Members of the second group were told that they would be subjected to a very light electrical impact. Then, all subjects were asked how they prefer the impact to be administered to them—in isolation or in a room with other participants. About two-thirds of the subjects of the first group expressed a desire to be with others. In the second group, about two-thirds of the subjects stated that they are indifferent to the anticipated impact—either alone or with others. The conclusion Schachter made was that, when a person meets any threatening factor, the group can provide a sense of psychological support and comfort. In the face of danger, people tend to be psychologically close to one another. This phenomenon is called *social facilitation*, which is the positive impact of the social environment on people's performance. Indeed, people need people!

It has long been observed that the social environment has its effect on the reduction of sensitivity to pain and noise, especially if under stressful conditions. Athletic competitions are examples of such conditions. There were many cases when injured athletes continued performing in spite of injuries without feeling pain. In the 1996 Olympic Games, American gymnast Kerri Strug was seriously injured performing her first vault. She needed not just to perform but to perform with a perfect score to advance her team into the first place. She visibly limped to the end of the runway for her second attempt. She saluted the judges and then ran as though it was not she who was limping moments ago. She performed her second vault, landed briefly on both feet and almost instantly hopping onto only her good foot saluting the judges. She then collapsed onto her knees and needed assistance off the landing platform. The coach carried her off the platform. Her score for the second vault guaranteed the Americans the gold medal.

The human ability to catch other people's emotions is experienced by many. Examples are spectators' group emotions at rock concerts or in athletic competitions and in other mass groups. Even watching, at home with friends, your favorite team play on TV causes elevated emotions compared to watching alone. The situation in the following example is from my past competitive gymnastics experience. It was not planned to be an experiment of the social environment's positive impact on performance but happened to be one accidentally. An elite-level gymnast took a semester off from his university study in order to dedicate maximum time and attention to his training before the upcoming competitive season. The coach agreed to work with the gymnast in his off time alone in an empty gym. It seemed like an ideal situation, a coach's undivided attention, no distractions—perfect. However, in about a week, the gymnast's interest in the training process declined, his emotional state worsened, and the stability of the learned skills worsened as well. Workouts became mechanical actions without emotional color. It was quite obvious that the cause of the recession in the gymnast's performance and emotional state was due to the absence of the social environment. After some discussion and reasoning, the coach decided to resume the gymnast's training in his "old time." As it turned out, it was the right decision. Next day, the gymnast entered the gym smiling, happy to see all his teammates and the usual working atmosphere. His training session that day could be referred to as a "blow" (or that he was at his best). The situation having changed dramatically, within a week he restored and improved his skills.

We should note, however, that sometimes the presence of others impairs the ability to perform. It may depend on personality features, particularly on the features of the nervous system; it may depend on the lack of experience and on some other factors. Zayonc (1966), in his experiments with pool players, observed that strong players sank more balls in the presence of others (70 up to 80 percent), whereas beginners and weaker players decreased the number of balls they sank (36 down to 25 percent). Stronger players were energized by the presence of onlookers, while weaker players were negatively affected by the presence of others during their performance. In this experiment, the negative effect on the weak players was due to the lack of experience.

Still, most of the time people perform better in the presence of others compared to performing alone. The presence of others activates energy, and people demonstrate better results in speed and strength, in endurance, and in other ways. In 1890 (yes, in 1890), psychologist N. Triplett (1898) conducted an experiment on cyclists. In the first series of the experiment, cyclists had to cycle on the stationary bike alone. In the second series, they cycled against a motor-driven stationary bicycle, and in the third series against other cyclists. The fastest speed they demonstrated—you guessed it—was in the presence of other cyclists: social facilitation at work, that is, a tendency to perform or work more effectively in the presence of others.

Small and Large Social Groups

Small Social Groups

From birth, humans live and act in small social groups. A small group is the aggregation of individuals who directly interact with one another by playing different social roles in order to achieve common goals, all the while being aware of their belonging to a given aggregation. An optimal size of small groups is five to nine people. If a group is larger, it usually breaks into subgroups. Examples of small groups are family, crew, athletic team, basic military unit, circle of friends, and the like. The importance of studying the dynamic of small groups is that the group members participate in joint activity and most often communicate face to face daily. The social process by which people interact in small groups is called *group dynamics*.[1]

From the social psychology perspective, not every gathering of individuals is called a group in the strict sense of the term. People riding a bus do not represent a group because they do not have a common goal. They are just random persons who happened to use public transportation to get to their destinations. However, if a violent act occurs, these people may join together in order to help one another and possible victims. In such a case, a distribution of roles will take place; some will take the initiative, others will follow. Thus, in order to consider a gathering of individuals a social group, three factors are necessary: place, time, and action.

There are countless numbers of groups—people involved in the lives of many small and large groups, both on a daily basis and in life. Regardless of the way a group is formed and whatever its objectives are, regardless of the duration of its existence and so on, a group is always something whole. Even a group of two people represents a sociopsychological unit in which each of them plays a different social role. For example, in the relationships of identical twins with practically identical biological features, an allocation of roles can be observed; one of them may act as a leader, while the other is a follower. A similar division of roles quite often takes place in the relations of spouses. The well-known playful proverb is an illustration of that: "The husband is the head and the wife is the neck. Where the neck turns, there the head looks."

Primary and Secondary Social Groups

All the diversity of social groups in the society can be divided mainly into *primary* and *secondary* groups. These definitions were proposed by psychologist Charles Cooley (1902). Primary groups are the contact groups, in which the interaction takes place on a daily basis, and their members are united by emotional closeness. Cooley called family the actual primary group because it is the first group for any human in which he falls into from birth. The family plays a pivotal role in the socialization of a human. Later on, psychologists began to call primary groups all those groups that are characterized by the interpersonal interaction. Examples of such groups can be a working crew, a departmental team, a group of friends, and the like. Only belonging to the primary group already has some value to its members because groups provide a certain satisfaction of needs for each member individually and for society as a whole.

For any primary group (small group), there is always a secondary group (large group) wherein the small group serves as its component. For example, shop–plant, crew–construction company, department–organization, class–school, sports team–sports club, and so on. Secondary groups are characterized by the impersonal interaction of their members, which is caused by various official organizational relationships. These groups are opposite to the primary ones in nature. The significance of the secondary groups' members to one another is determined on the basis not of their individual properties but rather of their skills in performing certain functions. People join the secondary groups primarily due to the pursuit of some economic, political, or other benefits. Examples of such groups are organizations, labor unions, political parties, athletic clubs, gangs of criminals, religious sects, among others.

Sometimes a person may find in the secondary group what she was deprived of in the primary group. Such a structure of society affects people's psychology and their behavior as members of small groups. Individual human behavior is consistent with the norms and value orientations of the group to which she consciously or unconsciously declares belonging to. One's spiritual and moral values can relate not only to the real secondary group in which the person physically involves but also to the so-called "reference group" group; for example, imitating manners of behavior or style of clothing of celebrities or following the lives of other admired individuals with whom a person has no face-to-face communication. It is important to emphasize that the social microenvironment that exists in real and in reference groups takes an intermediate position in the relationship of the individual and society. This microenvironment is never passive; it either enhances or weakens the influence of the society on the person. There are plenty of examples when people's mentality and actions coincide with the values of reference groups.

An impact of the secondary group on its members can be so strong that it may completely absorb the members' mentality. In some cases, it can even lead to tragic consequences. An example of such an absorbing impact on individuals by a group was the People's Temple in Jonestown, Guyana. The Temple's spiritual leader Jim Jones was successful in preaching a hostile view of American society and in achieving Temple members' submission to his influence. In 1978, California Congressman Leo Ryan visited the Temple with the purpose of surveying the Temple and interviewing its members. After reportedly having his life threatened by a Temple member, Ryan decided to cut his trip short and return to the United States with some Jonestown residents who wished to leave. As they boarded their plane, a group of Jones's guards opened fire, killing Congressman Ryan and four others. Following such an unexpected outcome, Jim Jones convinced his followers to make the ultimate sacrifice—to give their lives as a way to preserve the church. Nine hundred and twelve of Jones's followers were given a deadly concoction of a purple drink mixed with cyanide, and they all died.

Formal and Informal Groups and Social Roles

Formal and Informal Groups

People's relationships in small groups can be on the level of functional business contacts and on the level of psychological, human contacts. If a group is formed for a certain purpose—production, education, military, recreational activity, and the like—it is called a formal group. Examples of such groups are a factory shop, production unit, school class, an aircraft or a ship's crew, sports team and so on. Other groups are formed on the basis of personal relations, subjective feelings, sympathy, trust, common interests, and the like. These groups are called informal. For example, a group of friends is an informal group of persons who are pulled together perhaps by common amateur interests. The structure of any informal group in general is as follows: leader, followers, and isolated (rejected by the group or rejecting the group).

From the point of view of management, it is important to understand that psychological connections among people take place not only within informal groups. People build such informal connections by functioning in formal groups, in the groups that are formed for certain organizational goals. In every working unit, there are two structures—formal (official) and informal (unofficial)—and each of the structures has its respective formal and informal leaders. The formal leader obviously is someone who holds an official position—manager, supervisor, head of the department, military commander. The formal structure is designed by a business or an organization. It is based on formal rules and written instructions, where the circle of obligations for each employee is clearly defined. It also clearly identified who is accountable for what, who is subordinate to whom, and so on. Interpersonal relations within the formal structures are established on the basis of the generally accepted norms of conduct and controlled by regulations or orders.

Informal structure within the formal groups is a system of psychological connections among the group members. This structure is important for our discussion. Every production unit consists of people who are in the process of a joint activity project having psychological feelings toward one another—sympathy or antipathy, converge or diverge in tastes, personal interests, religious preferences, amateur affiliations. The manifestation of these feelings results in either mutual attraction or repulsion. Precisely these factors affect the emotional well-being of the team members, which influences their satisfaction in the workplace and ultimately their productivity. The effectiveness of group and individual performances is largely determined by the conformity of formal and informal structures. Simply put, if people at work evoke positive perceptions of one another, the process of activity runs more effectively against the background of positive emotions. The opposite can be observed as well. Informal groups can be identified by a number of factors—joint breaks, similar kinds of humor, similarity in the manner of dress. Most close friends in informal groups contain two or three people, although the optimal size can be up to seven or eight. Increasing the size of the informal group is constrained by the difficulty of everyday face-to-face communication. In larger groups, the existence of factions is inevitable, each with its own informal leader. Managers, as formal leaders, should be aware of the presence of informal communicative links among group members within the formal group structure.

Ignoring the existence of informal groups is not recommended because the most effective influence on the group members is through the group. Managers who recognize the power of informal groups and communicate with informal leaders, the most reputable members of informal groups, can only benefit. Leaders of informal groups are people who possess an informal authority that attracts group members to them. It can be their personality features or some specific expertise in a certain professional area or something else. Quite often their influence on the group is greater than that of the formal leader. Creating the desired psychological climate in the group is easier through the support of informal leaders. That's why managers ought to communicate with informal leaders in order to advance their organizational goals.

Be aware of the presence of informal leaders in your production unit. When necessary, try to influence the team members through them.

The ideal situation is when the formal and the informal leader are the same person. However, such overlap rarely takes place in real life because the informal leader may not always make a good formal leader. There are a number of reasons for that. First of all, the informal leader may have higher expertise only in some narrow technical field but, upon becoming the formal leader, faces a variety of fields to cover. Secondly, his personality may not be up to the requirements that are presented to the formal leader, particularly the ability to manage other people's activity. We will consider this specific phenomenon further in the book when we talk about the so-called "theory of incompetence".

Wouldn't it be easier for managers to work with the formal structure only and to ignore the informal one? It probably would; however, it cannot take place in real life because managers are not the ones who create the informal structure, and therefore they cannot just dismiss it. The sense of belonging to the informal group gives a worker certain status and recognition, creates the feeling of his relation to others; the feeling that he is somebody, even though in the formal structure he is just one of many. People go to work in anticipation of meeting friends and discussing with them not only organizational issues but things of personal interest—yesterday's game by the favorite team, sharing personal news, jokes, all of which generally eases the routines of working hours. The sense of belonging serves as some kind of an outlet for reducing the pressure of intensity in the workplace. If an employee is unhappy and feels she cannot talk to her boss about her problem, she knows that she can discuss it with friends. The benefit of the informal group gives its members a certain satisfaction and stability in the workplace, that is, it raises their level of psychological security.

Of course, the opposite may take place as well. The group may not accept a new formal member of the group into its informal circle of friendly communicative links, thus making her feel ostracized as an isolated group member. Such situations are very frustrating and may drive the person to seek a transfer or even to resign. Such dynamics can be vividly observed when a new employee joins the work group, but the invisible psychological shield of the informal group prevents him from acceptance. In order to become a part of the informal circle, the new worker has to be accepted by the group. Usually it does not happen on the first day of work; it may take weeks or may never take place at all.

The destruction of informal groups is very painful; changing the orientation of the informal group can bring more effective results. Soviet educator and writer Anton Makarenko (1985) promoted democratic ideas and principles in education theory and practice. In the aftermath of the Russian Revolution of 1917, he established self-supporting orphanages for street children, including juvenile delinquents left orphaned by the Russian Civil War of 1918–1920. In the orphanages, he succeeded in changing the orientation of the older street children. Makarenko gave them some authority by making them responsible for keeping order in the orphanages, for preventing bullying and other forms of violence, and for watching over younger members. Thus, he changed their orientation from being troubled themselves into his assistants in the orphanages and further in their lives into productive members of the society.

Social Roles We Play

> On the question who is the boss in the family a little boy said, "Papa . . ." Why do you think so? "Whenever I want my parents to buy me something or take me somewhere, I ask papa." And do you usually get what you want? "Yes . . . if mama allows."
>
> *A joke, unattributed*

Each and every one of us plays many social roles and generally in life by participating in different groups; for example, the role of a spouse and a parent in a family, the role of a manager at work, and the role of a leader in the circle of friends. Roles define our duties in the form of actions that we must perform in the eyes of others; it's what is expected from us in society. It arises as a result of the position we occupy in the social structure as we interact with other people. Indeed, as in Shakespeare's words "All the world's a stage. And all the men and women merely players. They have their exits and their entrances. And one man in his time plays many parts," we play our roles in life performing our duties, that is, what we feel we must do. For example, regardless of the manager's desire, she has to listen to the subordinate's complaint, who quite rightly expects her to do so. Respectively, parents must fulfill their parental responsibilities in the way society expects of them, and representatives of the law are expected to follow the laws and not be subjective in resolving legal matters. Roles allow us to navigate in the social stream determining who does what, when, and where. The roles help us to formulate our behavior so that we can blend our actions with the actions of others. We can say that the social roles are a sort of code or the reciprocal rights and duties of people in a society.

When the duties are determined by the rules, instructions, and so forth, they are formal expectations. In a formal environment, the manager's perception of his role and the employees' perception of the manager's role widely differ. Quite often, it creates an atmosphere of poor motivation and inefficiency. They may have difficulty communicating because they see things from different angles. For example, the manager may exercise a formal administrative approach toward employees, whereas employees prefer a more personal approach. Expectations based on the unwritten laws that most people follow unconsciously are informal. In conjunction with the notion that informal expectations are nowhere expressly recorded, people can interpret them differently, for example the way parents understand their responsibilities.

Professional roles that people play can impact on personality, especially if the role is performed for a long time. For example, elementary school teachers often transfer a simplified manner of presentation and explanatory voice intonation in conversations outside the classroom, even with adults. Or a military commander, who is accustomed to strict rules and regulations, transfers the features of formalism and dryness into personal relationships with friends, in the family, and with others. An example of that can be Colonel Frank Fitts, played by Chris Cooper in the movie *American Beauty*.

There are situations in life when performing one or more roles with prescribed sets of behavior can lead to so-called "role-playing conflicts". In other words, if a person is confronted by incompatible expectations of various social groups, she cannot meet one of the expectations without rejecting the other. There are two types of role conflict: between-the-roles and within-the-role. In the between-the-roles situation, an individual performs two or more different roles that present incompatible expectations. In such situations, a person feels "torn" between the roles. For example, the work duty requires spending more time at work, while the role of a spouse and parent requires dedicating more time and attention to the family. Or, in another example, the expectations of a student by the educational institution and parents might not meet the expectations of his friends wanting to spend more time in leisure and entertainment. The within-the-role situation occurs when an individual, while performing one role, is confronted by different expectations of two or more social groups. For example, a foreman must meet the expectations of his subordinate workers (vertically down) on the one hand, and his boss's expectations (vertically up) on the other hand. His subordinates and his boss have different expectations of his role, which can create a role conflict by placing him between the infamous rock and a hard place.

Such a situation may occur in private life as well. For example, when young people begin a new life as a married couple, it means that they enter into new social roles. This new situation is different from the one they were in of a boyfriend and a girlfriend. These new roles present new expectations. In these new circumstances with new responsibilities, they often discover the individual characteristics of each other, which they could not possibly know before they accepted the new responsibilities as a couple. This often introduces unexpected tension in relationships. Further, they now face the "eternal" issues related to the mother-in-law–son-in-law or mother-in-law–daughter-in-law relationship. One of the most frequent causes of relationship problems is different expectations of the opposite sides. An illustration of that can be the following joke. A woman is talking to her female friend about her married daughter and married son: "My son is a lucky guy, his wife adores him. She has a good paying job; she cooks, she keeps their place in order, and she always gets up first at night when their baby is crying. But my daughter is not that lucky. When her husband comes home from long hours of work, he expects the dinner on the table, he expects her to help him to keep their place in order, and to take turns in getting up when their baby is crying."

Role conflicts create stress and may even lead to tragic consequences. An example of that is an episode in a Soviet movie of yesteryear attributed to World War II.[2] A young SS officer, whose parents died when he was a little boy, was in charge of pushing the button to blow up Krakow, the capital of Poland. The resistance forces were able to approach the officer and revealed to him the truth about his parents. He now learns that those who raised him to become an SS officer were responsible for his parents' death. Learning the news, the officer felt trapped in a situation of a tremendously strong within-the-role conflict. He could no longer remain the person he was all the years of his life and, at the same time, could not just switch to the side of those who fought fascism. He resolved his role conflict by committing suicide. Whether a real or just a fictional episode in a movie plot, from the standpoint of social psychology, the result of such a role conflict has a well-founded explanation. Similarly, albeit not with such a tragic end, conflict situations may find themselves in children born of mixed marriages, where parents are of a different skin color, different ethnicities, or different religions.

The Compatibility Factor

> Do not marry a girl that does not laugh at a joke which seems funny to you.
> English proverb

A Group Is Not the Arithmetic Sum of Individuals

According to Aristotle, the whole is greater than the sum of its parts. No disrespect to Aristotle, but the sum of the parts does not automatically become a "greater whole" just because of the presence of the required parts. Not by chance, someone said about ancient Egypt's pyramids, "Those are not just bricks put together; it's about *how* they were put together." The same approach should be used with respect to the execution of tasks in a group environment. That is, not only the presence of needed specialists and their technical skills should be taken into account but also the degree of compatibility between them as well. Depending on the degree of compatibility, the result of group performance may either be equal to the sum of the results of individual performances or greater or lower than the sum. This suggests that the group is not the arithmetic sum of separate individuals but rather a single organism—a whole—and the result of the group performance is not always the positive sum of the results of individual performances by its members.

Representatives of various professions and other kinds of activity, such as polar explorers, mountain climbers, commanders of aircrafts and ships' crews, coaches of athletic teams, and many others, have experienced in real life that not all people are equally fit for complex teamwork. For example, a basketball team composed of individually technically strong but not compatible players—"stars"—can lose to technically weaker but compatible athletes composed into a team. This suggests the necessity of using a psychological approach in selecting people for teams in order to achieve maximum performance. What is the reason that some individuals who have sufficient knowledge and skills in a specific sphere of activity do not always perform effectively in a group environment? What is that special psychological approach that needs to be taken into account for the successful implementation of the group tasks? Let's consider some illustrative examples.

Is it enough to have a functional electronic device and the electrical network with relevant characteristics in order to use the device? The device and the electrical network are now components of the system electronic device–electrical network. For any system to function, the components of the system must be compatible. The availability of the functional device and functional network presents only the necessary condition for using the device. However, the sufficient condition for the device to be used is the compatibility of the device plug with the holes in the electrical outlet. As we know, the shape of the plugs and electrical outlets are different in different countries. If there is no compatibility between these two components, the device is impossible to use. Naturally, we neglect the option of disassembling the plug, baring the wire ends, and inserting them into the wall outlet.

Is it enough to have two persons and a serviceable stretcher for carrying a cargo? Two persons and a stretcher present only the necessary condition for such a task. One person, even physically strong, cannot do it alone; there is a need for two pairs of hands, so to say. Just like in the preceding example, these two persons and a stretcher are now components of the system person–stretcher–person. To satisfy the sufficient condition for performing the task, these two persons must be compatible by such parameters as height, physical strength, health condition, and so forth. If they sharply differ in these characteristics, the effectiveness of the system person–stretcher–person will either be very low or may even be equal to zero.

These illustrative examples shed light on the understanding that humans in the group appear in a new capacity, as components of the system member–other group members. A group may consist of the required number of specialists, each of whom possesses the necessary knowledge and skills but, in a condition of low degree of compatibility, will not perform efficiently. The lack of correspondence between the group members can be compared to a baby that learns to walk. Despite the fact that biologically a baby is a holistic organism—a whole—some "parts" of the child do not have sufficient functional correspondence. Therefore, the baby's movements are poorly coordinated; it staggers, falls. We can say that the baby, as a system, functions ineffectively. Similarly, we can observe the same kind of "malfunctioning" in a group performance. Thus, when staffing people for a group task, the compatibility factor should be taken into account in order to achieve the desired performance level.

An example of incompatibility can be a working crew where there is a significant difference in the skills of workers requiring coordinated application of muscular effort or relatively accurate movements. Another example is an athletic team formed of members with different skill levels. This kind of incompatibility is called physiological. In the preceding examples, such physical parameters as height, physical strength, motor skills, and the like are described. To note such differences in people is not that difficult, and it's unlikely that anyone will instruct people with such differences to perform a task where these differences present a hindrance. On the other hand, to put physiologically compatible people together for the task, performance will most likely bring the desired results.

People always experience a certain flow of feelings toward others within the group. These feelings are based on differences of a psychological nature, such as temperament, character, social orientation, habits, amateur interests, religious and national peculiarities and others. They may be positive or negative or neutral; they can be weak or strong in intensity; they can be mutual or nonmutual and therefore conflicting. These differences are not always obvious and apparent. However, particularly differences of this kind quite often have a decisive impact on compatibility,

Physiological compatibility

and, in turn, on the successful implementation of the group task. This type of incompatibility is regarded as psychological, and its presence is a major obstacle for effective group performance. The comic English proverb put forward as an epigraph to this section illustrates the incompatibility of this kind.

Thus, the level of compatibility/incompatibility may be influenced by a number of personality features. They may be purely physical, such as height and muscle strength, motor skills and physical development, health condition, and the like. They may also be communicative characteristics of personality, peculiarities of the emotional sphere, peculiarities of perception and attention, and so on. But mainly they are features of character as a combination of the most persistent mental traits that manifest themselves in activity. Generally speaking, group compatibility is characterized by friendly relations among members of the group, by the positive nature of emotional attitudes, by the pursuit of mutual cooperation, common interests, and needs, and by the absence of distinct selfishness. In other words, it's a complete fit of group members to one another. Thus, the factor of compatibility/incompatibility has a direct influence on group performance. That is, speaking in the language of psychology, "Two plus two is not always four."

Psychological incompatibility has its negative influence not only on the group performance but also on human health. Unfriendly, uptight relationships among group members in the working environment conjures up negative emotions. In mass professions where there are no exceptionally extreme conditions, people can perform productively under the influence of negative emotions for a fairly long time. However, performance comes with the cost of ongoing stress, until such time as relationships start to break down. Many can recall a depressing mental state due to incompatibility with colleagues or bosses at the current or previous job. Work activity against the background of negative emotions for a long period of time may cause pathological changes in the central nervous system, which could lead to various diseases of a neurotic order. People become irritable, experience headaches, insomnia, blood pressure disorders, dysfunction of the gastrointestinal tract, and other deviations in health. The typical medical approach for the treatment of such conditions does not always give positive results. There are statistical data in different countries on the loss of a huge number of work-hours as a result of the nervous breakdown due to psychological incompatibility.

Interconnected and Noninterconnected Group Activity

Group activity is also subdivided into the interconnected and noninterconnected. Examples of the interconnected group activity can be an airplane crew, a group of mountain climbers, or a basketball team. The main characteristic of the interconnected group activity is not only that each member has an assigned role but that these roles must be performed simultaneously. In interconnected group activity, the compatibility factor is of significant importance. An example of a noninterconnected group activity can be a group of designers working on a project where each member is working on a separate part of the project. The absence of one member of the group in a given moment does not affect the work of the group as a whole in most cases and, what is important, does not affect negatively on the group performance.

Psychological compatibility is the most crucial factor when activity takes place in extreme conditions. Examples of such conditions, among others, are danger, time limits, extremely cold or hot temperatures, and limited space for activity. In such conditions, fuzzy coordination among members of the group due to insufficient compatibility may endanger people's lives, particularly, for example, in the activity of aircraft and submarine crews, polar explorers, and mountain climbers. Athletic competitions, especially of high-class teams, are also examples of group activities in extreme conditions. The factor of compatibility in the described kinds of activity is an essential component in achieving the desired level of performance. The degree of psychological compatibility in these conditions influences the effectiveness of individual and group performance in both interconnected and noninterconnected group activities.

> In 1893, when the famous polar explorer Fridtjof Nansen[3] was getting ready to travel to the North Pole on foot, he had chosen as his assistant the most experienced navigator Frederick Johansen, who was the most reliable of the two dozen candidates. Johansen was also a lieutenant of the Norwegian Army, a man of calm and confident courage. Together they overcame many challenges and revealed themselves as good companions walking about one and a half years on the ice to the Pole. But they both began to annoy each other soon and quietly hated each other all the way. They communicated exclusively as needed, referring to each other as "Mister Chief of Expedition" and "Mister Chief Navigator." Even when a white bear attacked Johansen he did not retreat from the underlined business tone, "You should hurry up, Mister Chief of Expedition"—he referred to Nansen. And even after Nansen saved his assistant's life their relationship did not improve.

Hansen talked about their experience during the expedition in his lecture *What We Do Not Write in Our Books*. By the way, Nansen and Johansen did not possess conflicting personalities. An experienced explorer as Nansen would never have taken as an assistant a person who had a conflicting personality. In fact, the situation was just the opposite. Relationships between them could be called friendly, and the antagonism became evident only after they were "locked on each other" having been left without any connection with the rest of humanity.

As soon as these brave polar explorers returned to the fold of civilization and their endless 24-hour–everyday contact was ended, they became good friends again as they had been before the trip. That is, not even prolonged complete solitude with constant communication with the same person without having any choice can cause this kind of paradoxical effect. Of course, an office environment or a construction site is not the Arctic, and a colleague is not a polar bear, but still this classical example can serve as a reminder of the importance of psychological compatibility for performance. This factor should be taken into account whenever possible.

Can Interpersonal Relationships Be Measured?

There are methods of identifying and measuring interpersonal relationships among group members. Observation could be the first step for it, but there is another, more precise quantitative method. It's called *sociometry*. The method was developed by the American psychotherapist Jacob Moreno (1951) in his studies of the relationships between social structures and psychological well-being. Moreno called sociometry the means of "companion measure." He formulated it the following way: "[S]ociometry is dealing with the internal structure of social groups that can be compared with the nuclear nature of the atom or the physiological structure of the cell." Moreno claimed that the relationships among people based on the inherent ability in every human manifest spontaneous feelings of sympathy or antipathy to others. According to Moreno, people sympathetic to one another are able to communicate by means of a positively charged invisible *tele-factor*. People who are hostile to one another communicate by a negatively charged invisible *tele-factor*. Sociometry is based on the fact that people make choices in interpersonal relationships. Whenever people gather together, they make choices—who is perceived as friendly and who is not, and so on.

He studied the flow of these feelings in the work group by asking members to rank their choices of people with whom they would like to work or not to work. The questions could be related to work activity or to leisure. A simple example of sociometric analysis can be made on the basis of the nonthreatening *criteria* offered to group members of which they need to make a selection; for example, "Whom in the group would you choose to be seated next to at your workplace?" or "Whom in the group do you go to for advice on a work problem?" These choices demonstrate people's preferences in relationships between them and open the informal structure of the formal groups. Moreno developed the so-called "sociogram," a systematic method for graphically representing individuals in a group and the relationships between them. The purpose of sociograms is to build work teams based on people's preferences working together in order to achieve higher efficiency in the team's performance. A similar technique can be used for identifying the psychological closeness of the interpersonal relationships in children's groups. In such cases, the criteria could be: "Whom out of your classmates would you invite for your birthday party?"—or something of that nature. For younger children, it could be: "Please put a greeting card(s) into the box of a child (children) in our group whom you consider your friend," and so on. The sociometric analysis for both adults and children is done anonymously.

Moreno (1934) conducted his first long-range sociometric study in the 1930s at the New York State Training School for Girls in Hudson, New York. As a part of the study, Moreno used sociometric techniques to assign residents to various residential cottages. It was found that when the assignments were made on the basis of sociometric measurement, the number of runaways from the facility was substantially reduced. The important point of our discussion is that when people make choices in the working environment, it influences their state of mind and performance. Therefore, the awareness of the internal structure of the informal relations within the group is important for the successful implementation of managerial activity.

Another practical method for determining the degree of psychological compatibility is using the device called a *homeostat*. Originally, the device was created by William Ross Ashby,[4] an English psychiatrist and a pioneer of cybernetics. The device was adapted by the Russian psychiatrist and psychologist Feodor Gorbov (1968) for his work with Soviet cosmonauts (astronauts). This method is especially effective for measuring the psychological compatibility in the environment of extreme conditions.

Gorbov had gotten the idea for the use of the device by pure chance. He accidentally observed people taking a shower in a medical facility. There were four shower cabins, and the diameter of the water pipe apparently was not sufficient to ensure hot water delivery to all four cabins. Gorbov noticed that when all four cabins were in use at the same time, the behavior of each person identified a strategy aimed at creating the most favorable treatment for himself. When one of them tried to make hot water for himself without consideration about the others, the water flow to other cabins was not hot enough. This caused immediate reaction by all the others, who began rotating their handles trying to adjust the water temperature and, as a result, receiving either too hot or too cold water. Only mutual concessions eventually allowed adjusting water to an acceptable water temperature for all. In the event that someone quickly stood out and took the initiative, that is, took the role of a leader, the group could achieve the desired results faster. If the leadership was claimed by two or three people, it took much longer to have a reasonable water temperature for the group. Members of such a group were not able to regulate the water temperature by impeding one another; it either took longer time, or they could not perform the task at all. And, certainly, quite an impasse took place when one of them did not want to cooperate with others.

Later on when Gorbov used the "homeostat" for determining the level of compatibility of the group members, he observed similar results. The device consists of a control panel for the experimenter and a panel for the subjects. The task for each subject was to put the arrow in the zero position from a random starting position by using the remote switch. All subjects' panels were connected so that each subject's action affected the position of the arrows of the others. Each subject was allowed to look at only his panel while trying to adjust the position of the pointer arrow. Sometimes the groups were given unresolved tasks deliberately for the purpose of studying the behavior in conflict situations. Solvable tasks were used to evaluate the ability of the group to rapidly find a successful performance tactic. The groups were able to perform the tasks only if someone took the leadership initiative while the rest of the group acted under his influence, often unconsciously.

Social and Professional Adaptation and Psychological Security

The Adaptation Concept

From the moment of birth, humans must adapt to the surrounding physical and social environment. Air temperature, atmospheric pressure, plants, animals, and so on represent the physical environment. Categories and standards of conduct in the society, with its laws, customs, rules, culture, science, and religion, represent the social environment. In general terms, adaptation is the process of adjusting to the changing external environment. The adaptation process is aimed at maintaining the *homeostasis*, the tendency of the system (especially the physiological system of higher animals) to maintain the internal stability of the organism. That is, adaptation should be understood as the system of reactions of the organism's functional systems with an active and targeted goal aimed at maintaining homeostasis in the conditions of environmental exposure.

Though "adaptation" is a biological term, it found its broad application in other fields. There are three types of adaptation: physiological, psychological, and social. Physiological adaptation is the property of the human body to adapt its functions in accordance with the conditions of the environment. Psychological adaptation is the state of the person's adequate behavior to the changing condition of activity. Psychological adaptation can be seen more clearly in the case of psychological nonadaptation. An example of that is the state of tension that manifests itself in inadequate behavior caused by the complication of the conditions of activity. Social adaptation is the constant process of adaptation of the individual to the social environment, in general, and, more specifically, to new people in a professional setting—to the new team. Social adaptation is the prerequisite for effective interaction in the social environment.

The main criterion of adaptation is the degree of integration of the individual to the environment. If, in the process of interaction with the environment, the person is faced with information that contradicts the image of the real situation, a substantial mismatch between the mental image and the image of the real situation may take place. That is, the discrepancy between the subjective social-perceptual standard and the person's actual behavior is contrary to the attitudes and personality evaluation standards of the team; for example, "a teacher, but unfair" or "a military man, but undisciplined." Such situations are experienced as uncomfortable and, as a result, have their effects on the degree of adaptation.

Forms of Adaptation

A person who does not adapt to the society and does not accept its norms, rules, and laws cannot count on a decent chance of survival in it. There are two traditional forms of social adaptation: adaptation to the group's authority and adaptation of the group to one's authority. An individual is a product of an active and changing human environment to which she responds by adaptation and assimilation either by herself to it or by it to herself. In the first case, it is the conformal reaction, whereas in the second case, it is conviction, inspiration, and persuasion. In many cases, people adapt to one another on a parity basis, where social, professional, and other equalities among parties are taken into account, and no one forcibly makes others obey, and no one worships others. In such cases, the terms of coexistence or activity simply require people to show tolerance, affiliation, cooperation, assistance, and the like. Thus, there are actually three mechanisms of adaptation to the social environment (Moskvichev, 2003), as follows.

The adaptation of the individual to the group to its norms, rules, and patterns of behavior in connection with identification with it. In this case, we are talking about joining the society and adapting to new members. This is due to the necessity of understanding and acceptance of assigned roles and subordination. The identification with the group, respect for its rules and norms of behavior, and social acceptance are the main factors of entry into the group. The acceptance of a new member into the circle of people and his identification with them is one of the most important sociopsychological phenomena. For a new member, it is the basis for reduced anxiety about possible failures and other security concerns. It's worth mentioning, however, that the adaptation can go beyond the border of optimum level. In the event of an excessive "immersion" of the individual into the group, it may lead to the leveling of the person's own self, which could result in the loss of personal identity. If this kind of identification takes place, what is desired and proper coincides with the group's values and norms. For example, incorrect or ineffective solutions by the group are often the result of a group consciousness. This, in turn, can result in the suppression of the group members' intellectual activity. Group consciousness leads people to believe in the correctness of the decisions made by a group, even if they are against socially accepted moral standards and common sense.

Therefore, when talking about the group judgment, it is important to keep in mind the so-called "Abilene paradox". It has to do with what in social psychology is known as *conformity* and *social influence*. Sometimes people, who think contrary to the group opinion, feel stressed by not going along with the group.

Being afraid that the group may potentially express negative attitudes toward them, they go along with the group even though they do not agree with the group. If many group members will act the same way, it is very likely that the group can make a poor decision. One of the tragic consequences of Abilene paradox is considered to be the disaster of the American space shuttle *Challenger* in 1986 (Hughes and White, 2010). As the investigation of the causes of the disaster showed, just before the launch of the shuttle, the engineers warned their superiors that certain components—particularly the rubber O-rings that sealed the joints of the shuttle's solid rocket boosters—were vulnerable to low temperatures. If the decision was made by one person, he would probably have decided not to launch the *Challenger* at subzero temperatures because of the risk of the possible accident and the deaths of seven members of the crew. The commission, however, made the decision to go ahead with the launch, and *Challenger* lifted off. On the 73rd second after the liftoff, the disaster happened.

The adaptation of the inner circle and subordination of it to one's authority. This form of adaptation is more typical in the behavior of various leaders; it can manifest itself in two ways. On the one hand, it may be associated with authoritarianism—oppression, manipulation, and even violence. In such cases, it does not create an adequate relationship but rather suppresses initiative. As a rule, the adaptation of this kind is the desire to subjugate others to one's own interests. On the other hand, the subordination of others to one's authority can register in the minds of ordinary members as leadership in the achievement of group goals. That is, in this case, it has a positive outcome. With that said, it is important to underline that the power and passion to dominate takes place especially when there are sources and means of influence on others. Just the availability of them may cause a desire to influence their own kind.

In an experiment by Hekhauzen (1986), some subjects were given the status of managers, others that of subordinates. It has been observed that when they were allowed to impose sanctions on subordinates in a neutral situation, despite the fact that subordinates satisfactorily coped with their duties, it was twice as likely that managers would exercise their influence on the behavior of subordinates.

Another much stronger and well publicized experiment on exercising given power was conducted by a group of researchers led by Philip Zimbargo at Stanford University in 1971. Later on, a film was made based on the experiment. In the study of the psychological effects of becoming either a "prisoner" or a "prison guard," guards showed exaggerated manifestation of power over prisoners. They enforced authoritarian measures and ultimately subjected some of the prisoners to psychological torture. Many prisoners, at the request of the guards, readily harassed other prisoners who attempted to prevent it. Two of the prisoners quit the experiment early, and the entire experiment was abruptly stopped after only six days. Similar experiments were repeated in some other universities and schools in the United States and abroad. All of them resulted in similar outcomes.

These two forms of social adaptation do not cover cases where a mutual exchange of information, mutual care, responsibility, and control take place among equal partners. When adaptation to one another is based on parity, that is, when relationships develop spontaneously, parties are not subjected to anyone's will but somehow affect one another. This kind of control is different from the control sanctions being implemented through formal structures. This kind of control is implemented by people without someone's instructions. People, by being subjected to this voluntary control, act as its subjects and objects simultaneously. This is an important mechanism of self-regulated behavior in a group on the basis of which they adapt as equal partners.

If social integration is carried out on a parity basis, such things as the leveling of individuality, a group consciousness forced submission, and so on are not observed in comparison to the two previously considered traditional types. However, even in these cases, a certain "grinding" may be observed. But, most importantly, the peculiarity of their occurrence is that partners act as objects and subjects of influence simultaneously, and it is all based on the background of friendship, affection, and respect for one another. In general, it suggests that social interaction on an equal basis is really possible among people who are somehow interconnected and interdependent.

Professional Adaptation

Professional adaptation is the process of active adaptation of a person to the professional environment directed toward achieving a degree of compliance with the performance requirements of the professional group. It is a self-organizing system in which the main elements are the subject's structural components on the one hand and the features of the social environment on the other. Thus, professional adaptation can be defined as the process of "inclusion" into the new production environment. Even though the social and professional adaptation of the individual is different from the biological one, social and occupational factors (production environment, interpersonal relations, social networks, etc.) are also objective forms of impact on humans. The professional adaptability of a person manifests itself in two factors: the individual's adaptation resources and the parameters of the specific environment. The degree of adaptation reflects the effectiveness of individual social interaction within the group. It also defines the personality and characteristics of adaptive resources of the environment in which the individual's satisfaction of basic needs takes place. However, it is possible only if the results of the individual's activity relate to the requirements of the society.

One of the ways to facilitate the professional adaptation of new employees is by demonstrating individual attention. This method has been used in the past and proven as effective. During World War II, labor turnover at the Harwood Manufacturing Corporation plant in Marion, Virginia, was high. To solve the problem, a psychologist was called. The psychologist recommended giving individual attention to new employees upon their arrival. The main point of the program was to underline to the employees how their own jobs fit into the overall picture of the company production and that their significance is recognized by the company. In addition to an interview by a personnel department representative, each employee was assigned to an experienced worker, to a "counselor" of sorts, to whom the new employee could refer for any questions or advice. Thus, new employees did not feel isolated in their own world but rather felt a part of the new collective. Such a simple step elevated employees' feeling of importance as a part of the company. As a result, the administration was pleasantly surprised by the significant reduction in turnover.

Fast-forward to our times. In 2008, Facebook began using a similar and somewhat modernized version of individual attention. First, they established a program where all new employees, regardless of age and experience, had to go through a six-week induction process, through a boot camp program of sorts. That allowed new employees to learn all the computer codes of the company and to establish social bonding with other new arrivals. It was a very effective step from the social psychology prospective, namely, it created social bonding between members within the small group environment. The bond stayed with them in the future after each of them joined different teams. Second, the company assigned a small number of rotating senior engineers to serve as mentors who would meet with new engineers to help them adjust and to be more effective in their work. Also,

When new employees arrive at work, congratulate them. Inform them how important their work is in the overall affairs of the organization. Describe the requirements and point out the difficulties they may face in the process.

they put new employees into the rotating program, which enable them to get a broad experience and a global vision of the entire company. That was a really crucial part of the training. By going through the entire program, new employees got the feeling of a broad affiliation with the company, not just with their small production unit.

Psychological Security

Psychological security is one of the important factors of successful adaptation to the professional environment. Psychological security is understood as a certain protection of the person's consciousness against the different external influences, which may impact on the person's mental state, on her psychological characteristics and behavior that can dramatically affect the person, even including life-changing effects. Psychological security is characterized by a person feeling as though, "I belong here. These are my people, and this is where I want to be." It should be noted, however, that the process of "inclusion" into the professional activity is not something predefined. The formation of a person's psychological security and her adaptation to the environment do not coincide. Adaptation takes place significantly earlier. From the start, the person manifests as a passive object of adaptation. She is actively involved in adaptation only when a professional task is being accepted and acted upon.

There are cases when people do not accept the adaptation of professional life as their life task. It can be due to either an inadequate motivation and/or lack of required ability for performance or, on the other hand, the case of a very high level of abilities and skills that far exceeds the regulatory requirements of the objective conditions. In such cases, the formation of psychological security is difficult because the person is not satisfied with his work and with the prospects of professional activity due to the subjective (personal characteristics) and objective (environmental conditions) factors. Professional activity in such cases is perceived by the person as a heavy social responsibility and as a means only of solving financial problems. Then the person looks for other forms of self-fulfillment. There are instances of the reverse: The person is obsessed with the professional activity, which completely replaces his life. If the whole meaning of the person's life is in work, and, in the event that the work is lost, it corresponds to the loss of meaning of life. In such a case, objective environmental conditions (circumstances, a new boss, restructuring of activities, etc.) can cause the destruction of psychological security in the professional environment to which he has already been adapted.

The relationship between the process of professional adaptation and psychological security is tightly connected. The formation and development of psychological security are impossible without taking professional adaptation into account. Namely, within the framework of professional adaptation, a person forms a general readiness to working activity. The dynamics of the adaptation process has a direct impact on the formation of the person's psychological security. In general, the subject's psychological security in the working environment manifests itself in the degree of subjective feelings of satisfaction with the activity, in the ability to adapt to specific conditions and in the ability to perform the necessary professional tasks.

Thus, psychological security is characterized by the degree of satisfaction of the conditions of existence, especially satisfaction by the activity and by the level of resolution of contradiction between the needs and those conditions. It is primarily based on the subject's adaptability to the specific conditions of the technical and social environment and on the ability to perform the given professional tasks.

Chapter 4 in a Few Lines

1. The social environment is a prerequisite for the development of the human organism and of a person as a whole.
2. The social environment influences the development and formation of personality. The formation of such social qualities like interests, beliefs, attitudes, and the like depends on the kind of social environment a person is situated in.
3. Small social groups are the groups where people communicate on a face-to-face basis, playing different social roles in them. Performing two or more social roles with prescribed sets of behavior can lead to so-called "role-playing conflicts".
4. All the diversity of social groups in the society is divided mainly into primary and secondary groups. For any primary group (small group), there is always a secondary group (large group), where the small group serves as its component.
5. Formal groups are created on the basis of business contacts, whereas informal groups are united on the basis of personal relationships and mutual preference and trust.
6. A group is not the sum of individuals, and the result of group activities is not always a positive sum of the results of their activities.
7. Psychological compatibility between group members is the most crucial factor when activity takes place in extreme conditions. Psychological incompatibility has its negative influence not only on the group performance but also on the human health.
8. Social facilitation manifests itself in the form of a positive impact of the social environment on human performance.
9. Social adaptation is the constant process of adaptation of the individual to the social environment; in general—to new people, in a professional setting—to the new team.

Notes

1 German-born American psychologist Kurt Lewin was the founder of the group dynamics movement. He is often recognized as the founder of social psychology.
2 The title of the movie is *Major Vikhr* (1969).
3 Fridtjof Nansen, a Norwegian explorer and scientist, Nobel Peace Prize laureate.
4 W. R. Ashby, English psychiatrist and a pioneer of cybernetics, created the homeostat in 1948.

References

Cooley, C. H. (1902). *Human Nature and the Social Order. (Revised edn., 1922)*. New York: Charles Scribner's Sons.
Gorbov, F. (1968). Device for modeling the interconnected group activity. *Problems of Engineering Psychology*, 3, part 2. Moscow.
Hekhauzen, H. (1986). *Motivation and Activity*. Moscow: Pedagogika.
Hughes, P. and White, E. (September, 2010). The Space Shuttle Challenger disaster: A classic example of Groupthink. *Ethics & Critical Thinking Journal*, Issue 3, 63.
Makarenko, A. S. (1985). *Pedagogical Poem*. Selected works, Volume I. Kiev: Radianska Shkola.
Moreno, J. L. (1934). *Who Shall Survive? A New Approach to the Problem of Human Interrelations. (Revised edn., 1953)*. New York: Beacon House.
Moreno, J. L. (1951). *Sociometry, Experimental Method and the Science of Society: An Approach to a New Political Orientation*. New York: Beacon House.
Moskvichev, S. G. (2003). *Motivation, Activity and Management*. Kiev: Light Press.
Schachter, S. (1959). *The Psychology of Affiliation*. Stanford, CA: Stanford University Press.
Triplett, N. (1898). The dynamic factors in pace making and competition. *American Journal of Psychology*, 9, 507–533. Bloomington: Indiana University Press.
Zayonc, R. B. (1966). Social facilitation of dominant and subordinated responses. *Journal of Experimental Social Psychology*, 2, 160–168.

5

MANAGEMENT IS LIKE CONDUCTING AN ORCHESTRA

In everyday life, each and every one of us uses psychology in dealing with people, even though we are not always consciously aware of that. We respond to the behavior of others, we try to predict their reactions and build our relationships on that basis. We are guided by our experience, intuition, conventional wisdom, and so on. Some do it successfully, others suffer from their blunders. But if a person in a position to manage other people's activity makes blunders, they suffer from it too. The more people who come under that manager's command, the higher the cost will be of his psychological illiteracy to the organization or business and to society as a whole. Without taking the human element into account, achieving the desired objectives and maintaining people's satisfaction in the workplace for the long run do not seem possible. To work effectively with people, one must be prepared to think of them in human terms. People are filled with feelings, thoughts, and ideas, and they want to experience satisfaction with their implementation.

Managing Is Your Job

Managers Manage People

The main goal and the desire of any person in a position to manage other people's activity is to maximize their productivity. Without a doubt, machines, materials, and money are the basis of any industrial enterprise, but neither machines nor materials nor money can "work" without people. Managing people at work is not a part of the management process; managing people at work is the management as a whole. Regardless of the field of activity, managers work with people. A bank manager does not manage computers, safes, and accounts; a construction site manager does not manage machines and equipment; a basketball coach does not manage game tactics and techniques; a ship captain does not work the steering wheel but nevertheless gets to the desired destination by managing the ship's crew. Managers manage people!

Success in any business activity depends on the sort of relationships we have with other people, but in the field of management it is probably more significant than in any other fields of human activity. On the level of ordinary consciousness, each of us feels as psychologically perfectly fit and qualified on the basis of life experience to act as engineers of human souls. However, to manage people effectively in our modern times, some basic knowledge of psychology is a valued addition to the technical expertise in a chosen profession. To know peoples' individual differences, their ability to work in a group environment, as well as their values and expectations, their goals and desires, is essential for the effective implementation of managerial activity.

People live and act in various groups and are influenced by various formal and informal leaders: parents, teachers, older siblings in the family, managers, coaches, commanders, and others. Their personal traits and qualities, their behaviors and life styles as the dominant parties have a strong impact on people's mentality and play a significant role in their personal development. Many factors influence the psychological environment in the workplace, but the strongest one comes from the manager, from her managerial style. The way the manager relates to subordinates affects the whole nature of business communication and largely determines the group morale and the psychological atmosphere in the working environment. If the manager does not project a positive image her behavioral style automatically influences the relations among the team members. The working environment becomes stressful; people become less inclined to cooperate with one another, feeling uncomfortable and morally vulnerable. The group will break into subgroups, and consequently the team will cease to exist as such. All of that adds up on top of the "ordinary" work stress—intense workloads, deadlines, and other pressures.

That is why everything matters for the manager—the manner of handling communication with subordinates and other contacts, the degree of attention and courtesy, facial expression, body language, everything. All of that creates an overall background against which managerial activity unfolds. Of course, this should not be construed as a continuous idyll or as saying that the manager should not require subordinates to carry out their duties. Work is work, and business is business. When circumstances dictate orders and constructive instructions from the manager are justified, subordinates are expected to respond accordingly. They are aware that they will be held accountable for poor performance. The only thing they are not prepared for is a manager who does not notice their poor performance. If a subordinate does not perform as expected, you should let him know that you noticed it; otherwise he may get the impression that the omission will always be with impunity. Moreover, if you do not point it out to him, it says that you did not fulfill your managerial duties.

Subordinates expect you to lead. They are aware that they will be held accountable for poor performance. The only thing they are not prepared for is a manager who does not know what he wants and who does not notice their poor performance.

Teamwork

From the social psychology perspective, a team is a small social group of persons who are united and who cooperate to achieve a common goal. To work on creating a cohesive team is perhaps the most important thing for a manager to do in order to achieve the team objectives. For the successful functioning of the team, two factors are of the most importance: Team members must (1) possess the needed technical skills and experience in the field and (2) be compatible with one another. The first factor is well taken and understood, but the second one does not always get much attention. Creating compatibility is easier when each team member is at her respective level according to their best qualities.

Russian stand-up comedian Arkady Raikin once pronounced, "A good artist is someone who takes the right amount of paint and puts it on the right spot and as a result, creates his painting" (in Grigoriev, 1969). Accurately said! This should be a sort of a guide for managers for how to create an effective team, that is, to find the most appropriate role for each member. In a cohesive team, members complement one another because some people are good in some things, while others are good in something else. Hence, the Golden Rule in dealing with people: Do not try to change people; instead, learn to build on what they are and compensate for what they are not. Here is an illustration of such an approach. If a basketball player is good in shooting the ball but not as effective in defense, do not make him work on defense skills; work on the shooting.

Management Is like Conducting an Orchestra   77

To give a person the wrong role is like asking him to be what he is not. When he is pressed to be what he is not, he does not feel good and does not perform as effectively. But when he is placed where he feels "in his shoes," everything changes—he feels good, his productivity increases, and all the rest comes with it. Then people around him are amazed about the changes in him. But he has not changed, he became himself! It's worth repeating here Morris Viteles' credo mentioned in Chapter 1: "It is important that a man be kept out of a job for which he is not fitted. It is even more important that he be placed in a job where he can be efficient and happy."

Ken Blanchard, a management expert and speaker, the author of *Hi Five! The Magic of Working Together*, emphasizes the importance of teamwork. In his presentations, he always repeats, "None of us is as smart as all of us" and, "From the mentality 'I am the manager; you are my subordinates' to the mentality 'We all are one team.'" This kind of managerial approach encourages people to work with enthusiasm. After all, your subordinates' success is your success. If your unit performs well, you will be praised by your superiors regardless of who took the initiative and whose ideas were implemented in order to achieve the organizational goals.

Your team is your orchestra. You conduct its affairs, you direct and control your people's activity, you organize and coordinate their efforts, you excite and motivate them, and you are responsible for their performance. Hence, the manager should act as a conductor, not as a drill sergeant. An illustration of conducting

You should never make subordinates do the work that they are not good at. Strive to give each of them the tasks that best match their abilities and aptitudes.

this kind of management style can be the following; try to eliminate from your lexicon such commanding notes: "I want you to . . . ," "You have to . . . ," and so on. Instead, try to involve subordinates in the resolution of issues and problems; for example, "What do you think we can do to resolve this issue?" or "Here is a reason why I think you should do it this way."

Why is it important? Submission is rarely pleasant; any overbearing tone is perceived as a suppression of personality, as an encroachment on individual freedom. Demands for blind obedience and underestimating subordinates' initiative and abilities are perceived as abnormal and determines the corresponding attitude toward the manager. Requirements expressed in the form of proposals are perceived as more acceptable and tend to have a greater effect. By not showing your superiority, the discussion stays on an equal footing rather than issuing from your direct criticism and instructions. By acting in this manner, you show your respect to people, you value their competence, and psychologically you put them on the same level as you are. Such seemingly minor everyday things can either be an obstacle to the work progress or can serve as a "lubricant" in relations. The subordinate leaves with the feeling that you resolved the issue together and that her work or idea was appreciated.

We should note, however, that there are persons belonging to the category of followers; they are inclined to positive acceptance of the authoritarian guidance. They prefer to obey instead of taking responsibility.

To determine the effectiveness of a manager's work, ask: Can the team continue to operate smoothly and without disruption in his absence? Can they respond satisfactorily to customer needs? Can they provide superiors with the needed information? If the answers to these questions are positive, it's evidence that you're managing your team properly and that your team can continue to function productively in your absence. The size and the scope of the problems that subordinates can resolve by themselves are true measures of the success of the team that you have built. A teaching of the famous philosopher of ancient China, Lao-Tze, reads, "To lead people, walk beside them . . . As for the best leaders, the people do not notice their existence. . . . When the best leader's work is done the people say, 'We did it ourselves!'"

One Person Can Do the Work of One Person

> A little boy asks his mother why father often brings home his laptop computer and works late. Mother explains that father cannot finish his work in the office during the day and therefore needs to work at home after work. "Well," the boy said," why don't they transfer him into a slow group?"

One of the ways to get people actively involved is to delegate them a part of your power. Doing so is also a powerful motivational factor. It builds self-esteem and encourages them to do better in subsequent situations. By delegating, you can get much more done because "one person can do the work of one person." Sometimes you do need to work after working hours in your office or at home. However, if that happens often, it's a signal that you are doing something wrong. One of the possible reasons for this is that you are trying to do too many things yourself. Never forget that you are a manager, not a "doer." You manage, they do. Naturally, a "nondoer" does not mean that you don't have to do anything. Doing nothing in order to manage others is not an easy task. Sometimes it seems easier and faster to do much of the work yourself instead of teaching subordinates what to do and how to do it. Do not fall into such a trap; it will bog you down in details and make you lose the vision of the big picture. Doing the things that your subordinates should do will "suck" you into being a doer rather than being a manager.

There are some things that only you can do and your subordinates can't; there are many other things that they can and should do. Therefore, do only what you can do, not what they can and should do. Next time when you are going to do something, ask yourself, "Am I the only one who can do this?" If the answer is no, ask yourself another question, "Why then am I going to do it?" If the answer to the first question is yes, ask yourself, "When am I going to teach my people how to do it?" A Chinese proverb says, "If you give a man a fish, you feed him for a day. If you teach a man to fish, you feed him for a lifetime." In the same spirit, the essence of parenting is expressed in the Talmud in one sentence: "The father must teach his son to swim."

One person can do the work of one person. Transferring parts of your authority to subordinates is a way to stimulate them and to strengthen your power. Delegate!

If you do not delegate, your subordinates will never learn, and you will only blame yourself if something does not go the way you want it to go. The more you delegate, the more you will get done. Robert Heller (1998) writes:

> Many managers find it hard to delegate tasks because they feel insecure about losing control over the work or believe that giving responsibilities to subordinates will diminish their own importance. However, he continues, managers must work on eliminating barriers created by them in the matters of delegation, being aware that they are still responsible for carrying out the work, even if they do not do all the work themselves. Delegating to the right people should actually make them look better.

For those nervous about delegating, he suggests relying on the long known rule—the more you do it, the easier it gets.

In delegating, it's important to delegate a part of the project; delegate in accordance with people's individual personality features, their knowledge, and experience, and delegate the task that will help them to grow professionally. By delegating, you can concentrate on the parts of the work that only you can do. Organizing and directing the efforts of subordinates, you will greatly multiply the results of your own efforts.

If You Have Just Been Promoted to Manager

The main novelty facing new managers is the responsibility for the work of others and for making decisions not only for themselves but for their people. Linda Hill (1993), in her book *Becoming a Manager: Mastery of a New Identity*, notes that the typical discovery for new managers is that subordinates do not listen to them and continue to treat them as before. Instead of feeling free, they feel as they are trapped, "Before I was independent, was responsible for myself only, but now all these people can make my life miserable." Now you have to motivate your people and set an example in carrying out your duties before demanding the same from subordinates. Try to remember all your former and current bosses and consider all that they have done good and bad, all you liked and did not like about them. After such mental gymnastics, you may come up with the list of what you should and should not do to become an effective manager.

New managers also ought to realize that their new official position does not imply that they possess leadership qualities. The manager is obviously someone whose position is based on the vested administrative rights of the organization or business, whereas a leader is someone who possesses a high degree of influence on the team members by the virtue of her personality. Sometimes the most effective leaders in the organization are informal leaders, ordinary workers or employees without a formal position. The most favorable situation is when the formal and informal leaders are the same person; however, in reality such a coincidence rarely takes place. Due to the differences in objective requirements to formal and informal leaders, not every informal leader will make an effective formal leader. The informal leader, despite his high professional skills, credibility, and trust, may not possess the organizational skills, may not be demanding of others, and so on. For example, not every talented engineer can be an effective team leader, not every outstanding athlete can be a good coach.

If you have recently become the boss, try to identify the methods that your predecessor used in management. Take the best of his managerial methods and do not be in a hurry to change everything. Drastic changes may set people up against you because changes always bring additional stress. Thrive to create an atmosphere where your subordinates will feel their importance to the company. Share your plans with them, ask for their opinions, ask questions, but do not overdo it in this department. Establish contact with the subordinates, but that does not mean breeding familiarity. Do not make any of them favorites and keep a fair attitude toward each. It's enough to let them know that you know each team member's responsibilities and duties. Be aware of the presence of the informal leaders in your production unit. Try to make them your partners psychologically because the overall psychological state of the formal group (the team) largely depends on the relationships between the manager and the informal leaders.

When the relationships between the manager and the informal leader are positive, the presence of informal leaders does not prevent the flow of the team activity but rather improves it. When the situation is the opposite, the group may

Be aware of the presence of informal leaders in your production unit. When necessary, try to influence the team members' activity through them.

experience adverse consequences, such as malfunctions and ill effects. Further, if the manager loses his trust because of the inability to manage people properly, he may still keep his formal position by the support of his superiors. However, if he wants, for example, to sanction a team member by keeping only formal communication with her, it may have no effect because the team will express moral support to the sanctioned member. In contrast, if the manager is a true leader and will do the same, then the group, being in solidarity with him will behave as he does. The sanctioned member will find himself in a "vacuum" of only official communication with the group, which can have a stronger impact than any formal sanction.

One of the essential qualities of any person in the position of managing other people is to learn to perceive daily activities and sudden situations not as obstacles but as yet other opportunities to demonstrate knowledge, skills, and creativity. Work on the development of this quality in yourself. It will help you achieve your goals and objectives. When a problem occurs, the very first thing to do is to take a deep breath and ask yourself, "What are the possible ways out of the situation?" Consider all solutions, even those that seem unrealistic at first sight. It's like conducting a brainstorm with yourself. By playing in your mind the most unusual options, you may come up with the right solution to your problem or concern.

An important point for administration after promoting a specialist to a managerial position is to follow up on how the newly promoted is doing as a manager. Quite often, administrations anticipate that newly promoted managers know how to be managers; however, the reality is that it is not always the case. In most instances, they don't know how to be managers, and typically they will not ask for help themselves, being afraid that it might be understood as incompetence. Bosses are the ones who must encourage new managers and help them to deal with the new emotional pressure and stress. In 1994, the American Bureau of Labor Statistics interviewed the bosses of 230,000 managers and managers themselves who lost their jobs within six months after being promoted. The findings of the interviews indicated that the main reason why these new managers were fired was that they did not have a clear understanding of their duties. Bosses of the newly promoted managers must have been in the position to initiate such communication to newly promoted managers. If those 230,000 managers had taken the time to articulate a well-defined agreement about mutual expectations with their superiors, they might have kept their jobs (Levine, 1998).

They Want Good Bosses

What Is Your Management Style?

In the world of management today, many different management styles and their variations can be distinguished. Some authors identify five styles, others six; some even describe as many as 13 management styles. The styles also have different names depending on the authors. Regardless of the number of styles and terminology, the main thing when talking about management styles is to follow how managers make decisions and how they relate to their people. Some managers demand that subordinates obey their instructions with no explanation or discussion, whereas others encourage subordinates' initiative and active involvement in the problem solving and decision making. That is, basically we are talking about two opposite approaches (with some variations in the degree of their manifestation) in relation to subordinates.

Representatives of the former are basically characterized by the desire for excessive centralization of power, the exaggeration of the role of administrative methods, and the sole solution of most questions without discussing them with subordinates. They prefer being away from subordinates most of the time, not always informing them about the ultimate goals and other issues. They are recognized by the authoritative tone of voice, by categorical judgments, by brevity in communication with subordinates. They prefer to minimize contact among the group members, so all communication is passed through them and controlled by them. Such an atmosphere often creates preconditions for aggression and leads to intragroup conflicts, tension, and hostility in the relationship. The consequence of that is rivalry between the group members because of the desire to be "closer" to the manager. Such a group atmosphere often prevents a healthy spirit of cooperation and mutual trust. In the absence of the manager, the group members do not have the cemented base and may find themselves in a chaotic situation.

Representatives of the latter are characterized by allowing group members into coordinated activities and by maximizing their involvement in a joint definition of group goals. These managers do not seek a concentration of power and communication but rather vice versa; they try to delegate responsibility to the informal leaders of the group. They try to eliminate intragroup tension and conflicts, encourage and strengthen interpersonal communication. The structure of communication under such managers is significantly different from the structure of communication under authoritarian managers. This management style creates the precondition for more stable dynamics of activity of the group members.

The most important thing about these two opposite approaches in management styles is that both styles are good to use depending on the specifics of the team activity, on the situation, and on other factors. This can be illustrated by the following example. If the subordinate is competent and well aware of her responsibilities, the use of the authoritative approach would not be justified; this subordinate is mostly in need of support and positive motivation. In the opposite case, if the subordinate does not have sufficient knowledge and experience, the manager's clear directive instructions and oversight will intensify her activities. If the manager limits his action in relation to this particular subordinate to friendly support only, it will do no good.

Another management style differs from either of these styles. It's called "liberal" or "passive" by different authors or "chaotic" by others. Managers practicing this style are usually people who are not very knowledgeable in the field and often take the position to advance the self-serving tactical goal to "jump" to a different position in the near future. Or they are people who are conscientious and responsible by nature but with the features of inertness. The management activity of such managers is reduced to transferring the directives from above down and to function as observers and collectors of information. They allow subordinates maximum independence in the performance of their work. This management style cannot be effective in the production environment, in power structures, or in collectives where the activity takes place in extreme conditions. However, this style is quite acceptable in activity where control and guidance is not necessary; for example, the activity of the teaching staff in university departments, in scientific institutions, and everywhere else where creativity is the essence of the work.

Do Not Compete with Your Subordinates

An important factor that has a profound effect on the relationship between the manager and the team members is how the manager portrays herself in front of her people. Unfortunately, sometimes people who are in a position to confer power and control the work of others automatically believe that their knowledge and skills are superior to those whom they manage. Believing in their omniscience, they behave accordingly, that is, demonstrate their power where they need to and where they don't. Subordinates may possess more in-depth knowledge and more profound expertise and extensive experience in the specific field of a given profession. If the manager depicts herself as a know-it-all, she negatively impacts the flow of the team activity and most likely incurs people's dissatisfaction working under such a manager.

At this juncture, I would like to use an example from my personal experience as a manager of construction projects. Years ago, I was involved in the

Do not depict yourself as a know-it-all. Doing so negatively impacts the flow of the team activity and most likely incur an atmosphere of dissatisfaction working under such a manager.

Aircraft Noise Insulation Project representing a construction company. The project addressed all of the homes impacted by the aircraft noise from San Francisco International Airport. The Aviation Administration provided funds to the cities nearby the airport for performing sound insulation work in residential homes within the noise contour. A young architect was in charge of providing drawings for the project. An experienced general contractor, hired by the city upon his successful bidding, was in charge of the actual installation work. Inasmuch as the architect usually inspects the installation work, the situation appeared to be that this young architect became, in a sense, a superior to the contractor.

From the architectural and construction point of view, the project was quite simple. In particular, doors and windows had to be replaced by sound-absorbing ones, and some other installation work had to be performed as well. While reviewing the drawings, we found that a number of details were evidence of irrational decisions. Without going into the technical details, I will use only one example as an illustration. The entry doors of the houses and the doors separating the living areas from garages had to be replaced; only the doors, without the doorframes. It was an irrational decision. The houses were built about 40–50 years prior to this project. To install heavy acoustical doors into the light and slightly warped and aged doorframes and to achieve the needed sound insulation to the desired degree was next to impossible. The rational alternative would be to install new doors with new doorframes. It would be more effective and more efficient for two reasons. First, fitting the doors into the doorframes in factory conditions would allow for creating the closest fit. Second, the installation of doors on the site would require fewer work-hours.

At our first opportunity, we tried to draw the architect's attention to the matter. The response was, "Do as it's described in the specifications." We appealed to the project administrator and got in response, "I am not an architect." Then followed meetings and bureaucratic correspondence with the City officials, project administrator, and architect was the next unfortunate stage of the project. When the installation work was finally completed, the architect showed himself in all his glory—he demonstrated his dissatisfaction in everything we did. As a result of the turmoil, the project took much longer to complete than anticipated. All of this happened for one and only one reason: The architect did not have the courage to recognize that the general contractor subordinated to him offered more rational decisions. Had the architect cooperated in correcting the mistakes, none of this would have happened. The project would have been completed on time and to the mutual satisfaction of all parties.

Managers who at all costs try to show their omniscience often get into a "thicket," running the risk of demonstrating even more profound ignorance. Steve Brown (1985), the author of the book *13 Fatal Errors Managers Make and How You Can Avoid Them*, writes about three important words in manager's work: "The weak manager never says, I don't know. Instead he responds, let me get back to you on that"—and wastes half a day trying to ferret out the answer in order to save face. The manager who in response to a question for which he does not have an answer says, "You've posed an important question, and we need to know the answer; see if you can get it from one of the specific sources"—and sends an employee back to work with guidance, encouragement, and a compliment in the bargain. Such a manager has shown his emotional maturity and receives respect." So instead of "beating your own chest," just do the right thing. Do not compete with your subordinates!

People Are Not Just Performers

> No man treats a motorcar as foolishly as he treats another human being. When the car will not go, he does not attribute its annoying behavior to sin; he does not say, "You are a wicked motorcar, and I shall not give you any more petrol until you go." He attempts to find out what is wrong and set it right.
>
> Bertrand Russell, 1957

Frederick Taylor, mentioned in Chapter 1, considered the good worker as someone whose job is just to do what he was told to do. We live in a different era, and this kind of management style is not acceptable today. It may sound trivial, but a person can be employed only as a whole person. People's skills do not exist separately from their background and knowledge. Their personal lives are not totally separable from their work lives, and their emotional states do not exist separately from their physical beings. Each affects each other. When the boss responds to something personal and important to the subordinate, either to an exciting or sad event, with empathy and encouragement, it can make a lasting impression.

> Years ago an acquaintance of mine, a factory foreman, told me a little story from his work experience. A worker in his shop asked for an unscheduled day off due to some family circumstances. Upon learning the reason why the worker needed a day off, the foreman allowed him to take ... two days off. The foreman had no college degree but understood human psychology and therefore was a good manager. Subsequently, that worker has successfully worked in the shop as a crew leader.

The success of any enterprise is based on building good personal relationships between employers and employees, between managers and subordinates. The results of many surveys in evaluating managers of various fields of activity show that the ability to consider subordinates' opinions, fairness, tact, sensitivity, and the like are necessary for success in management. Human qualities are a necessary complement to technical knowledge for the effective implementation of managerial activity. If the administration cares more about managers' business qualities, subordinates expect of them both the technical skills and qualities of a psychological nature. People are not some abstract creatures but people with ascribed characteristics. They behave differently because they have different heredity and experience. Some are sociable, others are closed. They can be in a good or bad mood; the work can "burn in their hands" or "fall out of their hands." They may have personal aspirations and interests that do not match organizational objectives.

Former CBS executive Barbara Corday writes how important it is for managers to know their people:

> I have always been very pleased and happy and proud of the fact that I not only know all the people who work for me, but I know their husbands' and wives' names and I know their children's names, and I know who's been sick, and I know what to ask. That's what special to me in a work atmosphere. I think that's what people appreciate, and that's why they want to be there, and that's why they are loyal, and that's why they care about what they are doing. And, I think that is peculiarly female.
>
> *(as cited in Bennis, 2003)*

Well, actually any manager who treats her people not as performers only but as people possesses such a personality feature regardless of gender. In fact, years ago while working on the previously mentioned Aircraft Noise Insulation Project, I met a resident of one of the houses where we performed the installation work. The guy happened to be a supermarket shift manager. His relationships with subordinates were just like of Barbara Corday's. His position was, so to say, a classic example of the managerial position. Under the man's supervision were more than 100 people—fish and meat cutters, truck drivers, cashiers, workers at the packaging department, and others. He was in face-to-face contact with them practically daily, even though each department had its own supervisor. Naturally, I was curious to find out how he coordinated the work of so many people with such a wide variety of functions, how he resolved their relationship issues. What he told me confirmed once again the importance of taking the human element into account in managing people. He replied:

> Most of them began working with me in their twenties. They call me dad even though many of them are only about 15 years younger. I am always interested in their lives outside work and know practically everything about them—family relations, situation with children, financial problems and so on. I understand, if the employee has personal problems or the child is ill, or he's simply in a bad mood it definitely affects the performance. I always try to make myself available to talk and offer my assistance. I value their relationship and do my best to respond to their expectations accordingly. If you treat your subordinates not only as performers, but as people, they appreciate it and enjoy working under your supervision.

The man himself had gone from being a supermarket laborer working in different departments and gaining his own hands-on experience as to what works and what doesn't. People are not performers only!

Make Them Feel Important

> The deepest urge of human nature is the desire to be important.
> *John Dewey (as cited in Schul, 1975)*

It seems that these words were written for managers. When someone made you feel important and special, most likely you experienced the warmest feelings toward that someone. It is natural to try your very best after that. Taking time outside your office to greet people and making small talk in a friendly and genuine manner will let them know that they are important and valued. Appreciate people's abilities, admire their strengths and talents, and you will see what kind of response you will find in their soul. It is not so hard to see individuality in all people and make them feel important. People thrive in an atmosphere of acceptance and recognition, and sometimes they open gifts and talents in themselves, the presence of which they had not even suspected.

Two things motivate people stronger than anything else: achievements and acknowledgment of achievements by their superiors. John Dewey's quotation is worth repeating, "The deepest urge of human nature is the desire to be important." People want recognition, they want to experience their importance. They want to have their ideas considered and want to feel a real sense of accomplishment.

In the recent movie *The Intern*, there is a scene in which the boss's assistant Becky (played by Christina Scherer) burst into tears, complaining that with her

People are filled with thoughts and ideas. They want them to be considered and implemented. Consult with your subordinates, and let them experience their importance.

"business degree from Penn" she could help the company in many different ways. But the boss (played by Anne Hathaway) never asks her to do anything useful and hardly even notices her. Only when the intern (a 70-year-old intern played by Robert De Niro), while presenting an important analysis of marketing and sales to the boss, which he and Becky did together, reminded her that Becky has a "business degree from Penn," did the boss say she would talk to her. This is a good illustration of what we are talking about. Namely, everyone has a natural need for working activity and not just for generating an income but for work that brings satisfaction out of the work process and from the achieved results.

Employees want to know that bosses convey the same messages upward that they do to their subordinates. They want to know that bosses are advocating for them, representing the team and not just themselves. Bosses receive awards for the team's performance regardless of who is credited more. Nothing oppresses people more than the boss taking all the credit; nothing inspires people more than recognition of their participation in the team's success. Good bosses never miss an opportunity to get their employees' work on the organization's "display," and they do not feel intimidated when their subordinates look like heroes. Share the limelight with your subordinates, and you will receive their allegiance and enthusiasm in return.

The important factor in delivering recognition is that it must be delivered in a timely fashion in front of other people. Don't wait for some official event to mark the employee's contribution to the team success. Make all possible efforts to note people's merits when they expect it. It's called positive reinforcement, which tends to increase the probability that the act will occur again. Do not wait for the completion of the project to recognize the subordinate's good work. Break the

Share the limelight with subordinates. Nothing inspires people more than recognition of their participation in the team's success. Nothing discourages them more than the boss taking all the credit.

task into several parts and acknowledge the employee's performance for each of the completed parts. Even a little recognition can go a long way. Announcing at a meeting that the employee has done something special or presenting a handwritten note from a higher superior or any other way of acknowledgment plays an important role in encouraging employees to continue performing. Even if the success was achieved mainly because of your actions, congratulate your people. After all, it is they who carried out your instructions.

The Power of Words

Words Can Treat, Words Can Hurt

> Whatever is begun with anger ends in shame.
>
> Benjamin Franklin

Plenty of studies and simple life observations demonstrate that words comprise an immense strength and have a strong impact on human behavior, mood, and health in general. A remark can be made in a kind way or in a negative manner. Depending on the person to whom the negative remark is directed, it may either trigger an aggressive reaction in response or stay on the person's mind for a long time. The same remark made kindly without harming the human psyche can be more useful because it does not call for a defensive reaction. One of the causes of atherosclerosis, angina, heart attack, and other similar disorders is long-term exposure to negative psychological stimuli. Harsh words are one such negative stimulus. The human body reacts to such impacts by sharp spasms of blood vessels, especially the coronary and brain vessels, which disrupts the normal blood flow to these most vital organs. As a result, the body functions are impaired and lead to prolonged periods of illness. There is statistical data in different countries suggesting that these kinds of diseases are among the most fatal.

You should never express your dissatisfaction in a state of anger. Doing that will make it difficult to correct the relationships in the future. Irritability and restlessness are undesirable characteristics for a manager. Keep such manifestations of your behavior under control; otherwise management will be a constant stress for you and a torture for your subordinates. Someone said, "Speak when you are angry and you will make the best speech of your life you will ever *regret*." A friend of mine, a retired top-level manager, used the so-called "ten-count technique". Before expressing his dissatisfaction with a subordinate's performance, in order to calm himself down, he counted to ten with his inner voice. Sometimes before making a reprimand, he even turned sideways to the subordinate to make it look as though he was looking for something on the desk.

The manager is responsible for maintaining good working relationships between herself and her subordinates (vertical contour) and among subordinates (horizontal contour). Creating a positive psychological climate in the workplace should be an important part of managerial activity. In creating such an environment, managers should strive to eliminate factors that negatively influence employees' emotional state. Regularly informing subordinates about the state of affairs in the unit and in the neighboring units, about changes in the company, and about other subjects is a simple step in creating a positive psychological climate. Conducting leisure activities outside working hours enables employees to communicate in an informal atmosphere, bringing people together and influencing

Irritability and restlessness are undesirable characteristics for a manager. Keep such manifestations of your behavior under control. Otherwise, management will be a constant stress for you and for your subordinates. If you get annoyed often and experience anxiety, leave the work of managing.

92 Management Is like Conducting an Orchestra

Don't lose self-control and try to keep calm at all times. Demonstrate enthusiasm even if you don't feel like it.

their relationships in a positive way. People in a good mood perform more effectively; their actions are more energetic and precise. People in a bad mood show a lack of concentration, experience early fatigue, make more errors.

While trying your best to maintain a positive psychological atmosphere in the workplace, you are a human being too. You may have your ups some days and your downs other days. However, you should try your best not to have your people go with the flow of your emotional state swings. Make all possible efforts to provide them with your "even keel" most of the time. Don't lose self-control and try to keep calm with people at all times. Demonstrate enthusiasm even if you don't feel like it.

Rewards and Sanctions

One of the important methods in creating a positive psychological atmosphere in the workplace is the correct use of rewards and sanctions. The system of rewards is called "stimulation." In ancient Rome, *stimuli* were sharp sticks that were used to prick donkeys to make them keep moving forward. In today's world, of course, stimulating is understood as invigoration for aspiring people with positive forces and as a reward. Even if the employee deserves "sanctions on a stick," it should be mixed with the proverbial carrot. Do not begin with an attack; use the so-called "sandwich technique" instead. Start with some praise; for example: "I know that you are a good worker, but this time something didn't work out right." Point out the mistake, explain how to correct it, and finish with the praise, if the nature of the omission allows so; for example, "I am sure that it won't happen again; if you need my help, I am available." Criticism and sanctions should not be abused; otherwise, they lose their effectiveness and only cause the employee's reluctance to work, loss of initiative, and a hidden anger toward the manager. The frequency of sanctions usually arises from not knowing the subordinates, their individual characteristics, personal and family problems, life plans, and other personal information about them.

Some managers think that if people fulfill their duty at work and receive compensation for it, they are completely satisfied and happy. It does not come to mind that it would be nice to let subordinates know that their work is appreciated. Noticing the negatives is in the order of things, but noting the good daily work does not seem important. More than monetary incentives are important to people; moral and psychological appreciations and support are important as well. Good words, positive gestures, engaging facial expressions, a smile are simple ways to encourage.

> My neighbor, a college student, got a summer job at a store. Once I asked him how he liked to work there. He said, the job is OK, the manager is not. I went on, "The guy never smiles and never says thank you, is that what it is?" His face expressed an undisguised surprise, "Do you know him?" I did not even know what store.

If the subordinate made an error or oversight, use such an opportunity to help instead of "poking a finger in his eye." For example, the subordinate comes late for work on more than one occasion. The typical reaction to this is, "What's going on?" or "If this is going to continue, then . . ." However, the proper reaction should be, "I've noticed that recently you're coming late for work. Can I help you with anything?" You can reserve the time for your comment on that for later, but such a reaction will be an unexpected surprise for the subordinate and may resolve the situation more effectively. Similarly, if the employee does an occasional wrongdoing (not life-threatening or criminal, of course), try not to ignore or avenge the mistake; instead, try to help her to learn from it. If you yourself said or did something wrong, admit it and apologize. When a powerful person apologizes the payback is credibility, provided the apology is sincere.

Former General Manager of Chrysler Corporation Lee Iacocca writes: "Management is nothing more than motivating other people" (1984). Praise is magic. Bob Nelson, the author of books on management, put it simply: "In the workplace, money and fair wages are clearly important, but when it comes to long-term employee happiness and loyalty, it's truly a case of 'you can't buy me love'. Business that takes such motivational steps benefit from productivity increases, and these benefits have been measured statistically. If you recognize and reward behavior, it tends to be repeated. If you ignore or punish it, it will tend to stop. In short, you get what you reward." Just the title of his latest book *1501 Ways to Reward Employees* says it by itself. The manner you communicate is not of less importance. When delivering recognition to a subordinate, instead of saying something generic like "Good job!" be specific and concrete about what he has done. When proposing your idea that is based on someone's previous idea, make sure you give the person credit.

You can use the praising method not only in dealing with subordinates but with your boss and in other situations in life. For example, working on a project, you found a better solution. You can approach your boss, saying, "I have a good idea how we can resolve the matter" or you can present it by saying, "I would like your opinion on an idea I have." In reality, you may not need the boss's blessing. However, by acting this way, you make your boss feel important. People like the feeling of importance, it makes them more open, and you can benefit from it. Such introductory phrases as, "What would you suggest regarding . . . ?" or "Whoever I asked said that you are the best person to talk to about . . ." and so on. Don't neglect the gatekeepers either; they are the people who control access to the decision makers. If you make your request in a nasty way, it can land your request on the bottom of the pile. But if you make the person feel important—for example, "I would like to ask for your advice, what would you recommend in my situation?"—amazing things can happen.

Communication Is the Key

Communication as Human Ability

Human behavior rarely occurs outside the social environment, unless, of course, it's the case of Robinson Crusoe or Ted Kaczynski, the Unabomber. Whether we like it or not, we have to coordinate our actions with the actions of others. The need to communicate is a fundamental human need. Some consider it an innate characteristic of human and higher animals that begins immediately after birth. Others believe that the need for communication arises in relation with natural needs, like food, warmth, sex, orientation in the changing environment, safety, and more. Some others are not limited to the recognition of the instrumental role of contact and emphasize that the development of communication originates in the process of its implementation. For example, for a newborn, communication with adults makes them the source of needed vital benefits.

Humans by working and socializing developed a special ability to communicate with one another. This ability is language in its various forms: audio, written, and sign. Language that is understood as consisting of words is the most common way to communicate. Computer language and other symbols can also be described as languages of communication, as well as some other forms of communication like gestures, facial expressions, signals, art forms, music, and the like. As previously mentioned, Russian physiologist Ivan Pavlov called the ability to communicate by means of language the second signal system (or the signals of signals), comparing it to the first signal system. The first signal system consists of signals in the form of external and internal irritations, perceived in the real world by the visual, auditory, and other receptors of the body. The real world for animals is perceived only by the first signal system. The availability of the second signal system allows humans to transfer knowledge and to profit from the knowledge of others.

Communication is the basis of human activity; it serves a vital purpose of establishing linkages and the cooperation of people. However, the process of communication is not restricted to the framework of a simple interaction between people and the clarification of some information. As one of the main functions of humans, communication is not only the process of sharing information, knowledge, and intellectual property but the way humans develop.

Strive for Clear Communication

> The airline executive took the pilot aside after he had just landed the plane. "I would like to draw your attention to the use of a better choice of words when communicating with passengers," the executive said. "What happened?" the pilot asked. "Well, just before the landing, you made an announcement: 'I would like to take this opportunity to say goodbye to you all.'"
>
> A joke

Communication is a two-way process, where both parties want to communicate; otherwise it is not communication. It's the process in which each party makes an effort to understand what the other party is trying to communicate. It's about sharing and paying attention to the needs of the person or people you are talking to. Stephen Covey (1989), in his book *The 7 Habits of Highly Effective People*, formulated it clearly in a few words as: "[S]eek first to understand, then be understood." Communication is a verbal (or electronic, etc.) exchange between two or more people, subject to all participants having an active role in the process. From the speaker's position, a message must be transmitted and delivered clearly. The listener, who takes delivery of the message, must be an active listener. Only when the listener clearly understands the message that the speaker intended to send can effective communication take place.

In some activities, the value of clear communication cannot be overestimated. For example, communication between pilots and air-traffic controllers is simply vital. If a command or confirmation of the command is not understood correctly by either of them, it may lead to serious and sometimes even tragic consequences. Here is a real-world example of how miscommunication between the air-traffic controller and pilot led to a tragic end.

> On March 5, 1973, an aircraft Boeing 747–249F of the Flying Tiger Line was on the way to the Kuala Lumpur Subang airport (KUL). The air-traffic controller gave the command to the pilot of the approaching aircraft: "Get into echelon (go down) "two-four-zero-zero" ("2400"). Because of the similarity in the pronunciation of numeral "2" and the preposition "to" in English language the pilot confirmed the command incorrectly. He responded: "OK, to four-zero-zero" ("To 400" sounds similar to "two-four-zero-zero"). The air-traffic controller did not catch the mistake and the aircraft crashed into a hill.
>
> *(Makarov and Voskoboynikov, 2011)*

Among recently introduced FAA rules and regulations, some commands were modified in order to prevent possible miscommunication. For example, they changed the air-traffic controller command "affirmative" to "affirm" because possible background noise in the microphone may cover the first part of the word, and the pilot may only hear the "tive," which may be understood as "negative." Another example of difficulties that pilots sometimes experience is in distinguishing "five" and "nine," so they began using the more distinct "fiver" and "niner." Some other commands were also modified (Makarov and Voskoboynikov, 2011).

Of course, in daily communication in the professional and business world, such extreme situations are very rare, but still proper and clear communication is necessary in any field of activity in order to avoid undesirable consequences. Here is another more serious example. As described in the *9/11 Commission Report Executive Summary*, some individual departments of the CIA and other intelligence services did not communicate prior to the event, thus the information so vital for the country was not acted upon.[1]

Such situations, though extreme, have an educational value. In ordinary everyday business affairs, clear and proper communication is the key for effective management. In 2009, after the financial crisis of 2005–2007, the government launched a program to help homeowners with their mortgages. Under the program, banks reduced the interest rate to qualified borrowers, and thus their monthly mortgage payments were reduced accordingly. Homeowners sighed with relief. But unfortunately that was not the end of the story. In some banks, the department that offered mortgage relief to homeowners failed to communicate with the department in charge of implementing foreclosure. As a result, there were cases when the foreclosure departments, seeing that homeowners were making payments lower than their original monthly amounts, assumed that they defaulted and . . . seized their properties.

The latter example is evidence of lack not only of communication but of competence as well. Communicative competence is the concurrent part of professional competence in a growing number of professions. Communication ability was always valued highly, and in today's professional world it is particularly important. Having verbal and nonverbal communication skills is a vital factor in the production environment. The ability to deliver ideas and thoughts to colleagues and the ability to listen to and understand opinions of others are essential factors in achieving success in business.

In 1969, researchers at Harvard University studied the case of 4,000 people who were fired within one year (Schul, 1975). They came to the following conclusion: 10%, or 400, people were fired because they could not perform, whereas 90%, or 3,600, of the total number had lost their jobs because they showed a limited ability to communicate with other people. Researchers at the Pittsburgh Institute of Technology reviewed the cases of 10,000 working people and came to a similar conclusion: 15% of success was attributed to their technical knowledge, while 85% had to do with personality traits, specifically the ability to successfully communicate with others.

The use of nonverbal signals is as important for effective communication as verbal signals. Demonstrate your attention and acceptance with body language, nod when you agree and when points are made, use hands and other nonverbal gestures, and so on. These minor body language signals reflect your undivided attention. Keep eye contact, paraphrase interlocutor's comments, and ask questions to be sure you understand each other because all of us humans have a subjective perception, and we see things differently. Being a good listener is a big part of effectively conducting the communication process.

One of the most common excuses for blunders of communication in management is, "I did not hear anything. I thought that everything was going well." Such a statement is clear evidence of the manager's rare and inefficient communication with subordinates. If subordinates are not getting regular check-ins of their work, they won't know if everything is going in the right direction. If the manager, on the other hand, is not getting regular feedback from subordinates, it will be difficult for her to track the progress of the work. Maintaining regular and accurate communication with all the people involved in the ongoing project is essential to ensuring the smooth flow of the work progress. That, in turn, allows anticipating possible missteps in advance and making the necessary corrections. In order to maintain such a business environment, managers must provide appropriate and timely information to subordinates, so that they will know what they should do, when they should do it, and what is expected from them in general in the framework of work requirements. In other words, make sure that what is known as "getting through to people" takes place.

Understanding is subjective; it occurs in the receiver's mind. The fact that the communicator transmitted the message and the receiver heard it does not mean that communication took place. Even when the receiver understood the instruction or information the way it's intended to be understood by the communicator, it does not constitute a completed communication process. Communication is not only the receipt and understanding of information; it is also an acceptance of it and action. It can be illustrated, humorously, by one of the *Seinfeld* episodes. Jerry and Elaine called a car rental service to reserve a car. When they arrived to pick up the car, they were told that no car is available. Jerry began complaining, to which the receptionist said with irritation, "We know how to take a reservation." Jerry immediately retorted, "You know how to take the reservation. You don't know how to ho-o-o-ld the reservation. And that's really the most important part of the reservation" (David and Masters, 1991).

One of the ways to facilitate the communication process in organizations in general is to remove an unnecessary layer in the communication structure. Sergio Marchionne, the current Chrysler and Fiat Chief Executive, is known for his collegial style of communication with people. He prefers to deal directly with managers and employees. When he first arrived at Fiat, he was shocked to notice that executives communicate with one another through their secretaries. Upon taking the position at Chrysler Corporation, one of the first things he did was to set up his office on the Engineering Department floor. During his interview on *60 Minutes* on March 25, 2012, he pointed to the now empty top-floor penthouse of the Chrysler building, which a chairman and three vice chairmen used to occupy.

Communication Barriers

The proper flow of communication in the organization is like the water flow in the plumbing system. When the plumbing system does not function properly, it impairs the system's efficiency. Similarly, when the process of communication in the organization does not flow properly it impairs the organization's functional efficiency. Specific categories of problems may arise during the communication process; they are referred to as *communication barriers*. There are different categories of communication barriers, and there are a number of reasons for them to occur. A language barrier, of course, is one of the very common types of such barriers. Using words another can't understand certainly stops your message from being conveyed. It applies not only to actual languages but to expressions, buzzwords, and jargon. If a person is not familiar with your language, the barrier results in misinterpretation.

> My fellow countryman immigrated to the United States from the former Soviet Union years ago. He was an experienced engineer but with very

> limited English. Soon after the arrival, he got his first job. Because of his inability to properly communicate with his boss and new colleagues, he was under intense pressure of being fired any day. As he completed his first drafting assignment, his boss showed it to a superior. The superior glanced at the drawings, shook the guy's hand, and said, "Learn how to be an expert." The word "learn" clearly stuck in his mind that he needed to learn something. Not understanding the favorable meaning of the superior's comment, he went home as soon as both bosses left the room. In a couple of hours, his boss called to find out why he left the workplace. The guy's son said, "Your boss said that my father needs to learn something." The boss growled in response, "Tell him to come back immediately!"

Situations like this are rather common for newcomers who lack language skills. Many get into similar and sometimes funny situations more than ones in the process of mastering the language.

> Another friend of mine, on one of his first days on the job in this country, experienced something different. One of his coworkers approached him and said something. From what the coworker said, he understood only two words: "pool" and "dollar." Next day he brought his swim trunks, thinking that they were going to a swimming pool together. In fact, they collected a dollar from each team member to buy lottery tickets in a pool.

The causes of communication barriers can be in the content and formal characteristics of the messages. These are phonetic, stylistic, semantic, and in the logic of its construction. The *phonetic barrier* is an obstacle created when participants of the communicative process either speak different dialects or have significant defects in speech and diction or construct distorted statements grammatically. In such situations, psychologists advise to use a personality approach to drop the barrier. For example, ask the person, "Please speak slower and calmer. I will understand you better." *Semantic barriers* arise when participants of the communicative process use the same words but are referring to different things. It has to do with jargon and slang, with the limited vocabulary of one of them, or it is caused by social, cultural, psychological, national, or religious differences. The way to overcome semantic barriers is to familiarize yourself with the meanings of words used by the other person.

Stylistic barriers occur when communicators have different styles of communication. For example, one of them might use such phrases as "You have to," "You are required to," "You should" and similar, but the recipient is not used to a mandatory communicative style and does not accept them. She prefers the opposite style of communication, like "Could you," "It is desirable that you," and other such language. *Logical barriers* occur when participants in communication can't find a common language. For example, each of them sees the situation or the problem from a different perspective. Also, logical barriers often arise from communicators' unequal views of thinking. For example, one has developed abstract thinking, while the other developed visual ability. Logical barriers may also occur because of the different levels in operation of mental activity. Different people use such operational thinking as comparison, analysis, abstraction, and others with varying degrees of depth; perhaps one delves into a detailed analysis of the problem while the other has a ready answer based on the surfaced information. The most effective way to overcome logical barriers, according to experts, is to try to understand the way the other person thinks, how he comes up with conclusions and what the differences are.

In direct face-to-face communication, the emergence of barriers to communication often has to do with the ability to listen. If you do not listen when the other person is talking, you will not be able to restate in your mind the information that the person has just transmitted. Consequently, you will not be able to give proper feedback, which is crucial for effective communication. In the opposite situation, if you do listen and give proper feedback, it generates favorable feelings and sets a prerequisite to mutual understanding and good relations.

To generalize, each of us has our own unique style of communication, which may also become a barrier in communication with others. It depends on personality features like temperament, character, education, occupation and other factors. Most likely the style has been formed over a long period of time, therefore it is difficult to change it. Similarly, for the other person to change the communication style is as difficult as it is for you. Therefore, if communication is an important part of the working activity, we just have to find the way to accept the other person's communication style, otherwise we will not be able to communicate. In other words, the proper way to address such an issue is simply to allow the other person to be different and to try to understand his position.

Communicative Types of Personality

Not all people are able to easily communicate with others. People's communicative properties are different, and, as a consequence, their preferences of communication with others are different too. Some people feel comfortable working shoulder to shoulder in groups; others prefer to work on individual assignments, some feel "in their shoes" when they lead others, while others feel comfortable being followers. In the 1970s, psychologists of Leningrad University (now St. Petersburg University, Russia) established the differences in people's communicative characteristics of personality. They revealed four fairly distinct types in terms of the abilities to communicate interpersonally: leaders, followers, individualists, collaborators.

- The *leading type* has a pronounced emphasis on the leading role in a group environment. These people can work efficiently in the conditions of controlling other group members.

- *Followers* are the type of people who tend to prefer voluntary subordination. People of this type can successfully participate in the group task under the leadership role of the more confident, independent, and competent member of the group. Such people are generally good performers; they are good in performing their work. Their relations with other group members are based on group influence; they feel comfortable acting "like others." By agreeing with the group, they are free from making decisions, which is not always an easy task.
- *Individualists* are people of the category that represents the type of behavior with pronounced individualistic emphasis. Individuals prefer to work on individual assignments; they do not aspire to leadership and cooperation. They can successfully work on their part of the group task, subject to exclusion from the group in relative solitude. We can say that, for such people, the group environment creates additional exertion.
- *Collaborating* types are people who aspire to work with other group members; they are open to cooperation and ready to follow others in reasonable solutions. Typically, people of collaborating type are good business partners.

The described communicative differences in people should be taken into account in the process of managing work groups. Imagine a group with two members who are of the leading type or a group consisting of followers and individualists. In the former case, conflicts between two leading members is very likely; in the latter case, an atmosphere of uncertainty and confusion. In both cases, the performance level will be negatively affected. In this connection, it makes more sense to assign persons of the individualist type for distinct tasks with minimal interaction with other group members. Individuals of the follower type will work effectively on direct assignments "from the top." Persons of the leading type should be used, respectively, to carry out organizational activities. Collaborating-type persons are good for joint activities with other members of the group on an equal footing.

Good Managers Are Good Listeners

Are You a Good Listener?

The classical Greek philosopher Socrates formulated a long time ago: "Nature has given us two ears, two eyes, but one tongue to the end that we should hear and see more than we speak." Mary Kay Ash, one of the most successful businesswomen in American history, seconded Socrates' approach to the art of listening. In her book, *Mary Kay on People Management* (1984), she writes: "Good managers are good listeners. God gave us two ears and one mouth. We have to listen twice as much as we talk. When you listen, you are 'killing two birds with one stone'—you are receiving necessary information and letting a person feel his or her importance."

Unfortunately, quite often those who do not belong to the category of good listeners believe that other people see things as they see them or, even worse, that other people should see things as they see them. People do not only *not* see things the way we see them, but they just can't see them the way we do. People are different; their perception of the world is different because they see the world through the lens of their unique individual personality. Therefore, before trying to convince people to think your way (which in your mind is the only right way), try to listen to what they say with an open mind and understanding. When people see that you are trying to understand how they perceive the situation, they become less aggressive, their reasoning is somewhat mitigated, they become more open to compromise and mutual agreement.

Do you really listen when people talk? Quiet often we think we listen. In reality, we listen to our inner voice instead of listening to what the other person says. We prepare our arguments in our mind and attack the counterparty as soon as we hear his first argument. Therefore, the first rule for being a good listener is to turn your inner voice off until your opponent finishes his thought. Do you think about something else when your opponent speaks? Show him maximum attention and respect, and you will benefit from it.

And do you read between the lines? What people are saying is only part of what they want to bring to you. The other part is the body language, tone of voice, and other nonverbal signals. By reading body language, you will really see what is on the person's mind. Do you demonstrate with your body language an understanding of what he or she is saying? Repeat the main points of what your opponent is saying; this way you show that you really listen.

Some important qualities of a good listener are to look at the person, respond with your body language, nod your head if you agree, show with your facial expression if don't agree, lean toward the person, ask her to repeat some points, and preface some of your remarks with, "As I understood it, you said . . ." or "As you correctly mentioned in your observation. . . ." Steven Brown, the author of the previously mentioned book *13 Fatal Errors Managers Make and How You Can Avoid Them*, writes, "When I was working on my book I asked several of my business colleagues, many of whom held high level managerial positions, what kind of advice they would give in a book if they were to write one. Almost all of them put on the top of the list "Learn how to be a good listener."

What Category of Listeners Do You Belong to?

Let us consider four conditional categories of listeners. You decide which category you belong to. The first category consists of those who appear to listen, but their thoughts are elsewhere. Their comments are far from the conversation because they do not hear what the opponent says. In a certain way, it looks like a kind of comical situation: The opponents do not interrupt each other, but neither of them hears what the other one is saying. They are interested only in what they want to say instead of hearing what the opponent is saying. As a result, none of the arguments becomes a prerequisite for agreement. The arguments are not being listened to; opponents are just trying to express their own. In other words, by projecting negative effects on each other, what looks like an intense dialogue, in fact, is not more than a barrier of communication in the form of an interesting monologue.

The second category of listeners is made up of those who attempt to jump into the conversation as soon as the opponent tries to grasp some air. They interrupt each other just to say what they want to say before the opponent finishes his thought. The third category of listeners is those who talk at the same time as the opponent talks; they do not let the opponent "open her mouth." They ask questions without hearing the answer and often answer their own questions themselves. Listeners of the fourth category are real listeners. They look directly at you; they follow up your thoughts and concentrate on what you are trying to say. They demonstrate their participation in the conversation by confirming your comments with their body language and facial expressions, either agreeing or disagreeing. They are the real listeners!

Chapter 5 in a Few Lines

1. Managing people is like conducting an orchestra; hence the manager has to act as a conductor, not as a drill sergeant.
2. Change from the mentality, "I am the boss, you are the subordinates" to the mentality "We all are one team."
3. Delegating allows you to devote the time and attention to those areas of work that only you can do. Delegating is also the way to motivate people.
4. To find the right place for each team member according to his best ability is the way to create an effective team. It also elevates people's satisfaction at the workplace and enhances productivity.
5. Words have an effect on the human psyche, on people's mood and health. You should never express your dissatisfaction in a state of anger.
6. If you get annoyed often and experience anxiety, leave the work of managing.
7. Strive for clear communication; do your best to "get through to people."
8. Good managers are good listeners. By active listening, you get the necessary information and let the speaker experience her importance.

Note

1 *9/11 Commission Report* is a public record.

References

Ash, M. K. (1984). *Mary Kay on People Management*. New York: Warner Books.
Bennis, W. (2003). *On Becoming a Leader*. New York: Basic Books.
Blanchard, K. H. and Bowles, S. B. (2000). *Hi Five! The Magic of Working Together*. New York: Harper Collins Publishers.
Brown, S. (1985). *13 Fatal Errors Managers Make and How to Avoid Them*. New York: Berkley Publishing Group.
Covey, S. R. (1989). *The 7 Habits of Highly Effective People*. New York: Fireside Book.
David, L. and Masters, B. (Writer) and Cherones, T. (Director). (December 4, 1991). The alternate side. In L. David, G. Shapiro and H. West (Producer), *Seinfeld*. West Hollywood, CA: Castle Rock Entertainment.
Grigoriev, M. (1969). *Yesterday, Today and Always*. Moscow: Mosfilm.
Heller, R. (1998). *How to Delegate*. New York: DK Publishing.
Hill, L. (1993). *Becoming a Manager: Mastery of a New Identity*. New York: Penguin.
Iacocca, L. with Novak, W. (1984). *Iacocca: An Autobiography*. New York: Bantam Books.
Levine, S. (November 22, 1998). Implied Agreements Can Lead to Confusion at Work. *San Francisco Examiner*.
Makarov, R. and Voskoboynikov, F. (2011). Methodology for teaching flight-specific English to nonnative English-speaking air-traffic controllers. In G. Z. Bedny and W. Karwowski (Eds.). *Human-Computers Interaction and Operators' Performance*, 277–304. Boca Raton, FL: Taylor & Francis.
Nelson, B. (2012). *1501 Ways to Reward Employees*. New York: Workman Publishing Company.
Russell, B. (1957). *Why I Am Not a Christian*. New York: A Touchstone Book.
Schul, B. D. (1975). *How to Be an Effective Group Leader*. Chicago: Nelson-Hall.

6
ADDITIONAL CONSIDERATIONS

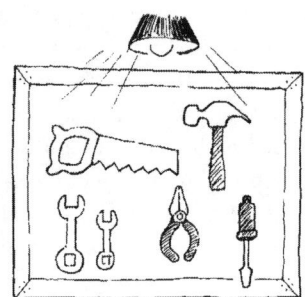

There are four topics in this chapter. Just like the tools in the handyman's truck, each of them has its applicable value. The first one is about the importance of preventing the step from the level of competence to the level of incompetence. The second is about some negotiation techniques. The third is about the theory and concept of stress and its manifestation in the work of managers. The fourth consists of some business tips for use in the practice of management and in business.

About Incompetence

Be aware . . .

Let's consider managerial positions, for example, a project manager. It does not need to be explained that the project manager needs to possess certain technical expertise in the given field of activity. However, the most important thing for the project manager is to be a good project manager because the main function of a manager is to manage people, that is, to possess the basic skills for implementing effective interactions among team members and with the "outsiders" of the team world—customers, consumers, clients—as well as the ability to predict and prevent high-risk psychological situations in the team activity. The requirements presented to the project manager sharply differ from the requirements that are presented to specialists. Accordingly, the question arises as to whether a good specialist, if promoted to the position of project manager, will be a good project manager. He may not possess the needed interpersonal skills to deal with people. If this factor is not taken into account and promotion is based on the person's performance merits in the present position, a competent specialist may become an incompetent project manager who is unhappy in the new role.

Now let's get introduced to the amazing theory of incompetence.

The Peter Principle

The concept of the theory of incompetence was brilliantly described by Peter and Hull (1969) in their book *The Peter Principle*, a humorous and yet very useful for practical purposes treatise. We believe it would be useful to get acquainted with this theory. Here is what Dr. Peter writes:

> Having formulated *The Principle*, I discovered that I had inadvertently founded a new science, hierarchiology, the study of hierarchies. The term hierarchy was originally used to describe the system of church government by priests graded into ranks. The contemporary meaning includes any organization whose members or employees are arranged in order of rank, grade or class. Hierarchiology, although a relatively recent discipline, appears to have great applicability to the fields of public and private administration.

The authors present an interesting theory that people progress through the ranks until they reach their level of incompetence. That is, as long as a person successfully copes with the responsibilities of the current position, she is a candidate for promotion. Indeed, it sounds logical that if an employee performs successfully, it's a prerequisite for promotion. However, as we will see in some examples from *The Peter Principle*, such a logical conclusion only sounds logical. In reality, an individual's successful performance in the current position does not necessarily mean that she will successfully cope with the responsibilities of the new higher position. According to the theory of incompetence, people are promoted as long as they demonstrate competent work in their current position. Sooner or later, they will be promoted to the position where they no longer will demonstrate a competent performance and thus will remain there, unable to perform effectively in their present position, having exceeded their level of competence. Right from the start, by reading the preface of the book, you will get the feeling of the sense and significance of the theory:

> By deciding to read the book you will never go back to the state of blissful ignorance. You'll never madly adore your superior and trample your subordinates. After defeating the incompetence in yourself and realizing its true nature in others, you will be able to better cope with your work, get promotions easier and earn more money. You could become a powerful man; you could help your friends and put down your enemies.... This knowledge will turn your life upside down and maybe save it.

The harmony of the theory of incompetence is amazing, but more importantly, "[A]fter reading about it you will see everything around you in an entirely new light." The theory of incompetence finds its reflection in any sphere of people's activity and at any level of the hierarchy. Look around and remember your current and former bosses, colleagues, subordinates. Remember where and when your order was not executed on time or executed poorly, what broke down or ran unsatisfactorily. All of that is the result of someone's incompetence. Dr. Peter collected thousands of real-life examples of people who reached their levels of incompetence.

One of the examples is about a young man who began working as an apprentice-mechanic in an auto shop. He demonstrated an amazing ability to pinpoint the malfunctions in a car's performance and showed patience in liquidating them. As a result of his work, he was promoted to a supervisor's position. However, in this position, his technical ability became interference to his duty as a supervisor. He personally got involved in every interesting repair when mechanics were standing by idly. He did not spend enough time in the office, and, as a result, orders were not executed in time. He could not find a common language with clients and with his mechanics. He was a competent mechanic and became an incompetent supervisor.

Another example is about a good school teacher. He was later promoted to the position of the vice-principal. He got along with teachers, students, and their parents. For his good work, he was promoted to principal. In the principal's post, he spent so much time on managing the school affairs that he did not have time for participation in various local societies and committees. The school lost public support, and he himself lost the favor of the school district superiors. When the district superintendent position became vacant, he was not recommended for that post. Thus, he would remain until retirement as an incompetent principal and an unhappy man. A competent vice principal became an incompetent principal.

And one more . . . about a general. Friendly deportment with subordinates, contempt for petty requirements of the regulations, and personal bravery made him the idol of the soldiers. Under his leadership, they scored many victories. When the general was promoted to field marshal, he had to deal with politicians and commanders in chief of the allied forces. He did not wish to abide by the accepted norms in their circles' diplomatic etiquette. He lost control of the war; control was transferred from his hands to his subordinates. Thus, his last promotion brought him to his level of incompetence. He was a competent general and became an incompetent field marshal.

The basic provisions of the Peter Principle are as follows:

- As a result of promotion, the employee can get to her level of incompetence. Sooner or later, it can happen to anyone.
- Competence on the current level automatically makes a person a candidate for further promotion. With time, every position will be filled by employees who are incompetent for performing the duty. For every individual, his last promotion will be the promotion from the level of competence to the level of incompetence.
- In reality, not all positions of the system are filled by incompetent individuals. In most cases, something is being done to achieve officially proclaimed goals of the given hierarchy. Someone has to "turn the wheels." It is done by those who have not yet reached their levels of incompetence.

What We Can Take from the Theory of Incompetence

1. The promotion of an employee to a new position means entering into a new role. In Chapter 4 we considered the concept of social roles. The new role always presents a new set of requirements, which most likely are very different from the ones the person used to respond to in his prior position. Therefore, if there is any doubt that a given employee will be able to meet the new expectations, then regardless of his merits in the current position, it might be more beneficial for both the company not to offer the promotion and/or the employee not to accept it. Ignoring this factor may bring the employee to his level of incompetence, and that is not a good place for anyone to be because to fail on the job is very damaging to a person's morale.
2. It is particularly important to give serious consideration before promoting a good specialist for a position where she will be managing other people's activity. It is necessary not only to explain to the candidate for promotion the requirements of the new position but to clearly emphasize how the new position differs from the current one, what kinds of questions will need to be resolved, what new contacts are included in the new sphere of business, and so on. But the main thing, of course, is to point out that the main difference in the requirements of the new position is to motivate *others*, to make

decisions for *others*, to be responsible for the performance of *others*, and to be an example in performing new duties before demanding the same from subordinates. This kind of information and consideration will help the candidate for promotion to be better prepared for the new managerial position or . . . will prevent her from stepping up to her level of incompetence. That is, sometimes it makes more sense to stay in the position of the "competent general."

3. Many people who become managers should not be ones, due to personality features that do not match the requirements of the new position. They agree to become managers because any promotion presupposes a salary increase, various privileges benefits. But precisely for the same reason, that is, by taking the step up to become the manager, they find themselves on their level of incompetence. In this regard, the question arises as to how to award talented employees who might not be suited for the position of managing other people—how to keep them motivated and satisfied in the workplace? One of the solutions is to find ways for material and other forms of award equivalent to the potential managerial post, for example, by creating a new position with a new title, such as consultant in the specific area of expertise or something of that nature. In such a case, this newly appointed specialist would report to the higher superior.

4. The Peter Principle should be in the back of the mind of all those who make decisions for promoting an employee to the managerial level or for promoting a low-level manager to a higher managerial position.

The Peter Principle can be considered one of the most outstanding sociopsychological discoveries of the 20th century, along with the discovery of formal and informal groups, the phenomenon of psychological compatibility, sociometry, and others.

A Brief Introduction to Negotiating

> Let's begin negotiation this way: You name the price that you want to pay, we both laugh, and then we'll talk business.
>
> A joke

Negotiation Is Not Arm Wrestling

In arm wrestling, one side always wins, the other side loses. Do you want to be the losing side? Obviously not; neither does the other side. Negotiation should not be a power struggle. In order to get what you want, it is not necessary to use power. Quite often negotiation heads toward a dead-end because each side focuses its attention on what each side wants. Sometimes a simple question like, "What can we do to improve the outcome of the negotiation?" or "What could change your position?" may open the door and turn the negotiation process in the direction of mutual satisfaction. Therefore, it is important to be imbued with the understanding of the important initial principle of negotiation: Negotiation is not arm wrestling but a mutual search for ways to give each side what each side wants to achieve.

Herb Cohen (1980), the author of the best-seller *You Can Negotiate Anything*, formulated it this way: "Nature made us all different; our needs are not the same. Thus, each side can be in a winning situation . . . if we can show the other side how they can get what they want and at the same time we get what we want." This is the only way to make people want to give you what you want when problems in the process of negotiation arise.

Negotiation, in a way, is a role-playing game where you should create mutual understanding, respect and trust. Always try to see the problem from the opposite side's point of view. The manner of your talk, the tone of your voice, the nonverbal signals you send should be directed toward convincing the other party that you understand their position. Try to avoid categorical statements in your comments and answers. When you say no, it immediately sets the barrier between you and your opponent. Starting your comments with, say, "If I am not mistaken, you said . . ." or "Your arguments sound very reasonable," you mitigate your response and diminish tension, as motor oil lubricates car engines. "He who treads softly, goes far," an ancient Chinese proverb goes.

The Let-Them-Speak Technique and a Few Others

It is easier to carry on negotiations if you know what is really on the other side's mind. Often the hardest part of the negotiation is the ability to listen. One of the classic rules of negotiation is whoever speaks first loses. People like to talk more than they like to listen, so encourage your opponents to talk. It will help you to better understand their position and thus will put you in a more favorable position. By letting your opponents talk and talk, they most likely will "give themselves away." The father of psychoanalysis, Sigmund Freud, scientifically described it as the so-called "unconscious slips of the tongue". The unconscious somehow always manages to make real feelings and thoughts known. If you patiently listen and display understanding of the opposite side's problem, you can even play as their team member in a sense. For example, you can react like this: "I understand where you are coming from, I don't know how to help you at this moment, but let me think about it." That is, in their eyes, you are trying to resolve *their* problem. You can say that you need to discuss their proposal with your boss or your partner. In reality, you may not need to, but in the eyes of the opponent you look as though you are trying to find a mutually acceptable solution. Coming back to the negotiation the next day after discussing the issues with your "boss" or your "partner" or over the phone, you can say that you were able to convince them on some points but that on some other points they did not agree. Then ask, "What can we do about it?" You are saying "we" on purpose to show that you are trying to find a compromise.

Don't be in a hurry to present your arguments while they talk; simply keep your mouth shut and listen. Do not rush to show a full understanding of what the other side offers. Let them feel that not everything is clear in their presentation. This will help you get a better deal. Moreover, do not start from agreeing to their terms from the beginning of the negotiation and hold on to some points that you are prepared to give up because the opposite side will demand more. When you give up on some points at the end of the negotiation, psychologically they feel as though they got what they wanted, and that will make them feel good. Therefore, sometimes it makes sense to purposely include some points into your proposal that you are prepared to give up at the critical stage of the negotiation.

Do not voluntarily inform your opponent about your time limit to complete negotiation because experienced negotiators will use it to their advantage. A friend of mine, a retired top-level manager of a big company, was sent to Japan to negotiate the contract on a serious matter. The very first thing they asked him upon his arrival was when was his flight back. During his stay there, they invited him for dinner more than once, took him on different tours around the city, offered different attractions, and so on. As to the contract, they discussed the terms on and off between the trips and dinners. Finally on his last day there, they said that they were preparing the final version of the contract and would bring it for his signature to his hotel. And they did. Scanning through the pages of the contract, he noticed several "discrepancies." Right then, in their presence, he called the airline to postpone the flight. They apologized for the "discrepancies" and within an hour brought new copies of the contract with all the corrections. Similarly but on a smaller scale, if you rush into an appliance store and say to a salesperson that your refrigerator is out of order and your food is getting rotten, you are not going to get a good deal.

People differ in terms of their personality features—by the manner and speed they talk, by religious and ethnic background, and so on. Most likely, your opponent is not like you. For example, perhaps you are quick and energetic by nature, and you can grasp a situation quickly and make fast decisions without getting into details. Your opponent may be just the opposite to you in her personality features or may be a detail-oriented person and needs more time and information for analyzing and making decision, and so on. Usually, people feel more comfortable dealing with the ones who have some similarity in personality. Try to "mirror" your opponent. If she speaks slowly, speak slowly too. If, in your opinion, she is taking too long to analyze the situation, do not make comments to that effect; it will not speed up the process but may just create the opposite effect. If your opponent is very scrupulous and pays attention to small details, do not say "somewhere around ten thousand"; say "nine thousand eight hundred seventy nine."

Upon completing the negotiation, compliment your opponent for her understanding and cooperation. Say that she conducted the negotiation in a highly professional manner representing her company and that it's been a real pleasure dealing with her. It does not cost you anything, but makes your opponent feel good.

The ancient Greek philosopher Socrates can be regarded as the founder of the contemporary art of negotiation. Information about how he succeeded in negotiations has reached us through time. Socrates never told his opponent that he is wrong; he never criticized him either. He never asked questions that could result in a yes-or-no answer. Socrates based his technique on agreeing with an opponent at the beginning and then asking questions to which the answers will be a yes. By receiving yes answers on his continuous chain of questions, Socrates led the opponent to agree on the crucial question, on which he could not agree moments before.

A yes-answer technique, for example, is used by companies that sell time-shares. Time-sharing is an arrangement between many owners to have the right to use a property under a time-share agreement. At the presentation, the salespeople usually show videos about the resort to the entire group and explain all the terms and conditions. Then an individual representative sits with each couple, answering their specific questions. Then the representative asks them the final question: "Would you like one or two weeks?" They get an affirmative answer from you without asking a yes-or-no question. They never ask if you like it or not or whether you want to buy it or not because that will require the alternative yes-or-no answer. A yes-answer technique is also a good way to schedule an appointment for offering a product or service. You always offer the person a choice of days and time, thus avoiding the alternative answer. You can say, "What time of the day is more convenient for you to meet me, before or after lunch?" If the answer is after lunch, again offer two days of the week, and so on.

Strive to Achieve a Win-Win Situation

Always try to structure negotiation in such a way so that both sides can win. Do not manipulate, do not use some kind of ingenious maneuvers. Do not underestimate your opponents; people experienced in business can easily spot your intention to mislead them. In many cases when parties cooperate, they both win. The winning outcome manifests itself in many different forms. Completing negotiation in a timely manner in a spirit of compromise and cooperation allows freeing the time, the manpower and equipment, and other resources for other deals.

Usually there are four possible outcomes from a negotiation: *win-win*, when both sides win; *win-lose*, when you win, the other side loses; *lose-win*, when you lose, the other side wins; and *lose-lose*, when both sides lose. All leading negotiators recommend achieving win–win solutions by trying to find the terms satisfactory for both sides. Let's consider some examples.

You are a manager or a business owner and need to fill a position in your team. If the compensation that the candidate would like to have is more than you have in mind but you agree, it's a *lose-win* situation. If the person desperately needs a job and agrees on the compensation that you offer, even if it's below what he expected, it is a *win-lose* situation. What can be done in order to create a win–win situation? Here is one of the ways to a win–win solution. You offer the compensation that is preferable to you but at the same time offer the candidate some benefits and other privileges as compensation. For example, allow him to work one or two days from home, if the specifics of the work allows it; offer bonuses, company stocks, additional vacation days, and the like. These additional benefits are either tax deductible for the company or do not cost anything today if the company's expenditures on what was offered were made a long time ago. For the hired person, these benefits compensate what he would otherwise have had to cover out of his own pocket. Of course, such privileges vary depending on the specifics of the company.

Another example: The department store magnate J. C. Penney opened his first store in 1902 as a one-third partner with two owners of the Golden Rule Merchant Company in Wyoming while working there as a salesman. Later on, the owners of the company made him a partner in two other stores as well. In 1907, he bought them out, taking over their three stores. He realized that it would be difficult to successfully manage and oversee all the stores by himself, even having a head manager in each store, because for managers it was only a job. So J.C. Penney implemented the principles used by his former partners, namely, allowing his store managers to buy a one-third partnership in new stores. Now he could rest assured that everything in the stores was under control because managers had a financial interest in the business. Later on, he expanded the chain based on the same principle.

An acquaintance of mine, a small business owner, knowing nothing about J. C. Penney, used a similar technique when he got involved in a second business, which required frequent traveling. He added some creative element to the technique, though. Namely, his manager now "pays" him an agreed-on fixed amount a month, and they split the profit in a certain ratio. Just like managers in J. C. Penney's stores, his manager is now trying his best because of his financial interest in the business.

And, finally, here is one more example of a win-win situation from my personal experience. Years ago, when I worked as a manager of construction projects, we put a newly constructed house on the market. The real estate market at the time was not favorable for sellers, so it took a while to find a buyer. The time for the completion of the transaction was anticipated to be about a month and a half. During the process of the buyers obtaining a loan, it appeared that they had some financial problems in the past that could prolong the transaction. It would definitely reduce the seller's potential profit because they continued paying interest on the construction loan, as well as carrying other expenses. They did not want to lose the buyers in such a slow market, and the buyers did not want to lose the opportunity to own the brand-new house. So the sellers offered them the opportunity to move in as tenants until the transaction could be completed. The buyers, a big family, were crowded in a small apartment, and even though their rent for the house was higher than they were paying for the apartment, they were very happy to move into their future new spacious house.

Practice Your Negotiation Skills Today

Not only politicians and businesspersons conduct negotiations. In our everyday lives, we negotiate more often that we think we do—at work, in the family environment, with friends and others. For example, discussing a rate increase with your boss is negotiation. Discussing the house chores with children in the family environment is negotiation—"If you want to get this, you will need to do this." Purchasing a refrigerator, a car, or a house is definitely a form of negotiation, and so on. Even in making arrangements for a picnic with friends, all the participants negotiate on when and where the picnic will take place and who does what, who will give a ride to whom, and so on. This negotiation is usually done to everyone's satisfaction. The point of this simplified example is to illustrate that achieving mutually satisfied results is easier when the needs of both negotiated sides are identified and satisfied.

Try not to delay practicing negotiation for some special occasions in the future. Begin to practice the skills in negotiation in your everyday life. Starting with things of small significance can be good practice. In stores, ask for discounts; call your telephone and cable companies and say that you are thinking about switching providers and ask whether they are willing to offer some promotional program. If you do not get a satisfactory result, call again to get to another representative; maybe he has more authority or is just more knowledgeable in the company's rules. When the time comes, try to negotiate on more serious matters, for example, when buying a new car. It is well-known that it is a good time to negotiate at the end of the year when dealers are getting new inventory but still have the inventory of the current year. After all points have been discussed and negotiated, ask the final question: "What extras can you offer to make me agree on the price?" You may get some extras.

At work, if an employee enters your office saying, "Hey boss, isn't it about time to increase my pay?" show your negotiation skills. Say that you may consider it but will ask for something extra in exchange. Try to use the same approach with your boss, "Boss, I would like to make more money. What should I do for that?" You don't ask for more money for nothing; you offer something in exchange. Dr. Chester Karrass, one of the best American negotiators, titled his book *In Business and in Life You Don't Get What You Deserve, You Get What You Negotiate*. It sounds like good advice.

The Stress Factor

The Concept and Theory of Stress

Stress! Who does not know this word today? However, long before stress became a commonly known word, changes in people's behavior in certain situations were described in the related literature as *psychic tension*, a mental condition triggered by the anticipation of adverse developments. As far back as during the Russo-Japanese War of 1904–1905, soldiers' mental and physical condition in anticipation of a battle was described (Shumkov, 1913). It manifested itself in unusual fussiness and in hypersensitivity to common stimuli—increased heart rate, frequent and uneven breathing, thirst, dryness of mouth and throat, less coordinated movements, altered handwriting, and so on. Similar kinds of symptoms are often experienced by athletes in anticipation of competitions. The condition is known as the so-called "prelaunch fever". A number of authors have shown that the effectiveness of people's performance under psychic tension depends on psychophysiological determinants, in particular of the features of the nervous system (Freeman, 1948).

In general, stress is a body reaction to different impacts. Our body reacts to these destructions with biochemical changes within the body, which in turn change its regular balance—homeostasis. The concept of stress was adopted by psychologists from physiology. Physiological stress is characterized by a violation of homeostasis and is triggered by the impact of an adverse stimulus (for example, the impact on the body by a sudden hit or extreme cold). The restoration of homeostatic sustainability after physiological stress occurs by means of a stereotyped chain of reactions. The analysis of psychological stress indicates a need to take such things into account as the significance of the situation for the subject and personality features. These psychological reactions determine the nature of the response because, between the external stimuli and the reactions, there are always some intermediate variables of psychological nature. For example, one subject may react to a threat with anger, another with fear, and so on. In most cases, the factors causing psychological stress are external influences—financial problems, work overload, family relations, mental frustration, and the like.

Thus, in contrast to physiological stress, in which the reaction is highly stereotyped, psychological stress is more characterized on the individual plane and cannot always be predicted. Behavioral symptoms of chronic stress manifest themselves in impatience, in interrupting others in conversations, in intolerance to minor obstacles, in general irritability, and in a lack of sense of humor.

The world's most famous researcher on the subject matter of stress, Hans Selye (1956), is known as the father of stress. He created the theory regarding the effect of stress on human capability to resist and adapt to injuries and diseases. For his scientific achievements in the theory of stress, he was called the "Einstein of medicine." Selye pointed out that stress is one of the normal processes of the body. Despite the fact that stress can be harmful to health, it does not mean that we should (or can) avoid stress. High emotion can cause the body's stress response; however, it's unlikely that we would like to give up the exciting emotional moments and events in our lives.

Selye made a deep analysis of changes in the body, particularly in the endocrine glands, under the influence of negative impacts. He discovered that patients with a variety of ailments manifested many similar symptoms, which he ultimately attributed to their bodies' efforts to respond to the stresses of being ill. Selye called this collection of symptoms the stress syndrome, or the *general adaptation syndrome* (GAS). In other words, our body reacts with similar biochemical changes to different stressors. Heat, cold, injury, or verbal threat, happiness or sadness—our body reacts with similar biochemical changes. Selye writes:

Stress plays a decisive and integral role in every business venture and in every business negotiation. Like heredity, high-fat diet, and lack of exercise, it can contribute to coronary disease, peptic ulcers, suicide, nervous disorders, migraine headaches, insomnia, pill popping, cocktail hang-ups, marital discord, child abuse, self-abuse, lack of confidence, allergies, strikes, picketing, and labor violence.

How Accountants "Helped" to Shed Light on the Nature of Stress

In 1957, Dr. Meyer Friedman (1984) conducted a very interesting experiment on the nature of stress. Participants were 40 accountants. The time of the experiment—between January and May—was chosen on purpose, namely, the period when accountants are busy preparing income tax returns for their clients. Dr. Freidman measured the blood cholesterol level and the speed at which their blood clotted. In January, February, and March these vital signs were completely normal. During these months, the accountants did not alter either their eating or exercise habits. During the first two weeks of April, however, as the tax-filing deadline approached, the accountants were desperately striving to finish their clients' tax forms and get them signed and in the mail. Their average blood cholesterol level rose abruptly, and their blood began clotting at a dangerously accelerated rate. In May and June, with no further deadline to face, the blood cholesterol and clotting times of these accountants returned to normal levels.

For the first time in medical history, a clear-cut demonstration of the power of the mind alone to alter man's blood cholesterol and clotting time had been achieved. When Dr. Friedman's colleague reported these findings at the annual meeting of the American Heart Association, there was no applause following the presentation, only a dead silence. To those scientists, Dr. Friedman wrote later on, who had spent almost their entire careers believing in the hypothesis that only what a person eats can affect his blood cholesterol level, the news was definitely shocking. It is not anymore.

Under stress, the body releases unhealthy hormones into the bloodstream, especially corticol. These hormones raise blood pressure and can lead to elevated cholesterol levels. They also make the blood more likely to clot. However, stress is not always harmful; it can play a positive role because under the influence of stress factors, our body produces the hormone adrenaline. As a result, our body receives an additional supply of oxygen and energy, which is of a vital importance in critical or life-threatening situations. However, if it happens often or takes place over an extended period of time, the body depletes its reserves, which leads to violations of the immune system,

Stress in the Work of Managers

When a person is promoted to the position of managing other people, the stress level increases. The main reason managers experience increased levels of stress compared to the stress experienced by nonmanagers is that managers are responsible for the work of others. And that is in addition to being responsible for her own performance for the capacity and variety of tasks, deadlines, for maintaining social contacts, and so on. Being under pressure as a part of their own work, managers experience demands from other managers who are above them. First-level managers (supervisors, foremen, group leaders) experience additional stress because of the significant circumstances of their position. They experience an impact of two diverse groups—their bosses (the managers) and their subordinates (the performers). Their position is unique in the sense that they have to satisfy the expectations of these two heterogeneous groups. That's why they feel themselves between a rock and a hard place, and that's why they get into role conflict situations more often. Their bosses' expectations are different from their subordinates' expectations. This circumstance makes the job of the low-level managers more stressful than the job of any higher-level managers. Any managers above them are in contact with two homogeneous groups: managers who are their subordinates and managers who are their bosses.

We live in an era of rapid social and technological progress. We cannot get away from the accelerated pace of the modern society; therefore the only way to survive is to find ways to reduce the effect of stress factors. In the group work environment, a variety of factors influence stress levels. However, the strongest of them comes from the manager's personal influence. Managers, not employees, are in the position to regulate the psychological climate in the work environment. Every manager, from the one on the lowest level to the one on the highest level, has to develop skills to control his own stress and to look for ways to reduce the influence of stressful factors on subordinates. Here are some simple recommendations to that effect.

Do not monopolize time during discussions; interrupt others at meetings; show your temper; look for a scapegoat if something goes wrong; lecture or criticize employees in front of others; reject compromise as a solution to problems; put yourself above other people.

Do respect other people's opinions; let other people state their opinions before you talk; listen to people with attention; react with verbal and nonverbal signals when people talk to you; give constructive advice; share information with people; encourage people and help them to succeed; show genuine interest in people's lives.

Among stress-reducing techniques are the well-known stress-busters—exercise, enjoying a hobby, and spending time with family and friends. Some people find relief in meditating. Prayers and time regularly spent in the religious community help to deal with stress as well. Among other preventive measures to fight stress are any kind of activities away from everyday routine duties—trips to the country, vacations far away from home, and so on.

Psychologist Wanda Mills experimented on some other preventive methods in stress reduction. In one of her studies of 275 female managers, she was able to conclude that women, who play several social roles (mother, wife, manager, and athlete) are much better equipped to deal with and resist stress than women who play only one or two roles. Mills gave the following explanation for the results of the experiment. When a woman finds herself in a stressful situation while playing one social role, she can focus on satisfaction by playing another social role or roles. For example, stress at work can be compensated by a warm family atmosphere or by a victory in an athletic competition. In other words, an active lifestyle helps the body resist potential negative impacts caused by stress.

A Few Business Tips

Do It Now!

In every job, in every business, there are always unpleasant things to do that we want to push aside for later or even try to avoid doing. It can be an unpleasant telephone call, a response to an e-mail, or just an unpleasant part of everyday duties. Pleasant things are easier to do, unpleasant are not so, but the postponement of the unpleasant tasks does not resolve anything. Unanswered phone calls and a bunch of e-mails to respond to are not going to disappear by themselves. To relieve yourself from the "headache" of keeping it in your mind, try to resolve the problem while it is still small and while it does not grow into a big one. Get these unpleasant elements of your work out of the way. Concentrate on the good feelings you will have and on the advantage it will bring to you by completing these unpleasant parts of your work.

As soon as the thought to do it later flashes in your mind, force yourself to do it right at that moment; do not procrastinate. Learn to do first the things that you don't want to do! Do yourself a favor: Hang a small poster saying "Do it now!" in a prominent place near your workplace. After a while doing it now will become a habit, and you will see how good you will feel following this simple "trick." Do it now!

About Partnership

Partnership statistics are rather sad. A large percentage of partnerships dissolve during the first year. The rest do not last for more than a few years. One of the major reasons for such sad statistics is the relations problem between the partners. Recall from the discussion about group dynamics in Chapter 4 that the effectiveness of a group performance is not always a positive sum of the performances of its members. The reason is that, in a group environment, each member functions not independently but rather as a component of the system member–other group members. In the new role as a partner, a person may manifest some "new" personality features in the eyes of the partner. But those are not new personality features; the person just did not have an occasion to manifest them. It may sound trivial, but even knowing someone for a long time, you cannot predict how he or she will act in the new relationship. So before entering into a partnership of any kind, try to remember your first impression of the person. Next, try to remember even the seemingly most insignificant episodes in your relationships, the other person's reactions and comments on different situations with you and with other people. It can be a great litmus test to determine the personality features of the person you are to go to get into business with. It may help to identify the person's undesirable qualities for the partnership and prevent you from entering into a potentially problematic business relationship. Do not base your decision on emotions; do not try to see what you want to see. "If there is a doubt, say no," as the American proverb goes. Such a thorough analysis of the person's reactions to people and events will help to determine your future partner's strengths, and that will be beneficial for the partnership.

If you are already in a partnership, do not act as a parent, do not patronize your partner. Upbringing ends in childhood; in adulthood, it is called self-upbringing, which only the person himself can do. Marilyn Ferguson, an American author, editor, and public speaker, put it smartly: "No one can persuade another to change. Each of us guards a gate of change that can only be opened from the inside. We cannot open the gate of another either by argument or emotional appeal" (1980). So let your partner express his or her individuality, treat them with respect, and demonstrate your patience. Do not be afraid to stress the qualities in which the other person is better than you; encourage the person to use these qualities for the sake of the partnership. Your partner will accept it with gratitude. It will "inflame" their partnership activity. In the end, it will be in your common interests.

There Are No Unimportant Details in Presentations

It is obvious that, when preparing for a presentation, you have to check not only the availability of all materials and the details of your presentation but also how you are going to use them. If during the presentation, you cannot find the needed document or display, if you discover that an electrical cord is damaged, if listeners cannot read the small text on the displayed tables or figures, if something is in the wrong order and you are trying to rearrange pages of the physical document or on the screen, it will definitely affect the quality of your presentation. In order to have your presentation a success, use the following tips. Even if some of the recommendations are in the category of common sense, they are still worth mentioning.

- Knowledge of the subject is without a doubt the most important thing. Specify the subject of your speech in your mind in a single sentence and then proceed to the preparation.
- Develop the topic during the presentation and at the end summarize what has been said or discussed, which must match what you formulated in your first statement.
- Try to find out as much information as you can about your listeners and structure your presentation accordingly.
- Dedicate the time to each part of your presentation in accordance to its importance.
- Rehearse if not all, at least some key points of your presentation. While rehearsing, try to cut the presentation by a few minutes less than the time dedicated to it. In reality, for some "mysterious" or unexpected reasons, your presentation may take a little longer than you planned.

- It's important to fit your presentation into the time allowed. Your listeners give you their time. Give them something useful in return. In the time when there were no watches with batteries, a joke about it went like this: If during the presentation, your listeners glance at their watches periodically, it's only half of the problem, but if they bring their watches close to their ears, you are in trouble.
- If it's a PowerPoint presentation, you can still have some paper notes with you, and it's OK to glance at them once in a while.
- Use the so-called "five-minute principle". Begin the presentation with some information that will attract the audience's attention. If you start your presentation with a boring or unnaturally energetic voice, your listeners may switch their attention to something else.
- During the presentation, try to find some friendly faces in the audience and focus on them as if you are talking to them.
- Put on some comfortable clothes that you have gotten used to. Avoid having a heavy meal before the presentation; otherwise your body will struggle with sleepiness. It is not recommended to drink cold water before and during the presentation, it may affect your vocal cords and lead to hoarseness.

About Business Letters

The ancient philosopher Socrates never wrote anything; we know his work through Plato's account of it. When asked why he did not write, Socrates said, "A sheet of paper cost more than what is written on it." Times are different; in our world we cannot exist without letters or in the business world without business letters. Along with the rapid development of means of communication, individual letters are, so to say, "keys of communication" among other instruments used in the business world. If in small businesses it is possible to communicate by personal contact, in big companies with a wide spectrum of production, letters play the role of personal contact.

Any letter should be considered as a dialog, as personal contact between the one who writes a letter and the one who will read it. That's why, before writing a business letter, try to imagine in your mind that you travel the distance necessary to talk to the person to whom you are going to write. Regardless of what you are trying "to say" in your letter, the language should be as if you met the person on the street or in his office. This way, your letter will be more effective. It is especially important if you are writing for the first time to someone who does not know you. It has the same effect as your first impression in person—your manners and so on. At this juncture, let's consider the most basic rules of writing business letters.

- Always be aware that you know what you are going to write about and the other person does not know. Try to write from this kind of perspective.

- Begin with the main thought that you are trying to deliver, so that the reader understands at once what you are trying to offer or what you are asking for.
- Concentrate on those to whom you are writing; think of who they are. Write as if you are talking to them.
- First describe the main point, then correct and edit if you feel the need. Start every new thought from a new paragraph.
- If you get stuck in the middle of a paragraph, skip it and go on. There is no need to write a letter in "one direction." Get back to the unfinished thought later.
- The letter should be laconic and easy to read. Try to use simple language. Remove the words that do not add anything to the main thought of your letter. Two short sentences are better than one long one.
- Sometimes you can write a whole letter in one sitting, as they say, but sometimes brief breaks help to fire up connections in your brain that can help to find better words.
- If it is possible, leave an unfinished letter aside for a while and come back to it later. It is especially important if you are writing while emotionally excited.
- When the letter is completed, scan the entire text, ignoring style and other possible roughness. The purpose of such a scanning is to follow the logic of what you are trying to deliver in your letter.

A well written letter does not leave uncertainty; it minimizes the number of errors in the process of conducting business and saves money. Individuals possessing the ability to "talk on paper" have additional value for the organization. Write so that what you write will "cost more than the paper on which your letter is written."

Do You Like Being Criticized?

Doubtfully. Do you like being criticized and to pay for it? Strange question, isn't it? However, as is well-known, everything is relative, and, depending how this issue is approached, it may not seem as strange. Companies often invite well paid consultants whose job is to search for the flaws in a company's operations, that is . . . to criticize.

At work, you may receive criticism from your subordinates or from your boss. Criticism from subordinates costs you nothing, but criticism from your boss may "cost" you. So it looks as though choosing the first option is wiser. Let your subordinates criticize you, that is, let them . . . make proposals on how to improve the operation in your unit. But in order to let them do that, you have to "get off the pedestal" and not fend the criticism. Otherwise, your subordinates will not criticize you; that is, they will not make any proposals. Think of their criticism as a free consultation. Think of their criticism as the early signals of irregularities in your work before the roughness in your work will be noted by your boss. So, when your subordinates express their opinions, do what you were taught in preschool: Do not interrupt when others are talking.

Moreover, show them with your facial expressions and gestures that you are listening carefully. And that is not all: repeat some of their comments. They know that you hear what they are saying, you know that they know, but these repetitions emphasize that you are listening with full attention and perceive what they say. You will receive useful information, and they will feel important. Encourage those who speak out against your opinion or express unconventional but useful ideas. Do not forget to thank them; it will encourage and liberate others. Implement their ideas and make changes in your management style based on the information obtained from them. It is not always easy, but this kind of open group atmosphere will have a positive effect on people's job satisfaction and will create prerequisites for improving the efficiency of their performance. Thus, improving your unit's performance based on the information you receive from subordinates will be to your benefit. And it will not "cost" you anything!

Criticism is something that is often associated with a negative experience. However, if you use criticism as a tool and not as a weapon, it may lead to mutual benefits. Late Vice President of American Airlines Walter Johnson, in a discussion about the benefits of positive criticism, illustrated this point with the following example:

> A pilot coming in for a landing is a good example of successful criticism. Frequently, his flying must be criticized or corrected by the tower. If he's off course, the tower doesn't hesitate to tell him so. If he's coming in too low, he's told about it. If he is going to overshoot the field, he is corrected. Yet I've never heard one of our pilots getting offended by this criticism. I've never heard one say, "Aw, he's always finding fault with my flying. Why can't he say something good for a change?" (as cited in Giblin, 1985)

Such criticism is not made to express superiority but to achieve a good mutual result.

This kind of criticism is called constructive as opposed to demoralizing, in which a person is criticized for no good reason. Criticize in essence, constructively, and do it as soon as the error occurs. Discuss with subordinates what can be done to prevent such a mistake in the future. Criticize as described in the example of the pilot. Make it a rule to praise more than criticize, using the sandwich technique. Criticize once for an error; don't come back to it at every opportunity. Always criticize the person in private, without the presence of others. Under no circumstances make generalizations of the kind, "What can we expect from you? You always . . . ." Point out only the specific error the subordinate made.

Encourage cooperation. Do not say, "Do it all over again, and I hope this time you will finally do it right" Instead, say, "Could you make such and such changes?" When you command, you put your subordinate in the position of inferiority. When you suggest, you include her in your team. End criticism in a friendly manner, "I know you can do it, I'm counting on you. . . ."

In summary is the quote from Randy Pausch, author of *The Last Lecture: Really Achieving Your Childhood Dreams*: "When you see yourself doing something badly and nobody is bothering to tell you anymore, that's a bad place to be. You may not want to hear it but your critics are often the ones telling you they still love you and care about you, and want to make you better."

How to Deal with Angry Customers

Communication with an angry person can be compared to two people walking on a narrow bridge toward each other. Each of them wants to get to their destination; neither of them wants to be thrown off the bridge. One of the most common causes of an angry tone is frustration. In most cases, the person on the other end associates you with the company you represent as if you personally are to blame. The customer is discouraged by the poor performance of your company, or so he believes. Maybe something was not delivered on time, or important information was not transferred, or an appliance that your company sold does not work properly. The customer is angry and feels somewhat neglected, which in his opinion justifies his state of mind and the tone of his voice. Or maybe the customer is just not an easy person. Whatever the reason, you are on one end of the phone line, and your task is to defuse the tension, to "put out the fire," so to say.

By responding to the person on the other end of the phone line, you in fact are entering into a negotiation. Earlier in this chapter, we talked about some ways of reaching a positive outcome in negotiations. That suggests that the first thing to do is not to react in unison to the angry person. The tone of voice in a verbal response is important. It has an effect on the tone of voice of the person you are trying to communicate with. Experiments were conducted to that effect, and it has been established that people fall under the influence of another person's tone of voice. When you say something in a loud voice, the response is in a loud voice as well. When you say something in a calm voice, the response is in a similar manner. This says that it's possible to bring the other person's tone of voice into the state of tranquility and transform an angry person into a calm one. It is possible to monitor your own emotions and the emotions of other people to an astonishing degree. Experiment with that yourself, and you will see that it really works.

Because psychologically the person on the other end is prepared for possible objections on your part, you should do the opposite, that is, let the person speak. Let him "let off some steam"! Your patience in listening will help to defuse the tension. Usually, this alone may partially solve the problem. In a calm and restrained tone, say something like this: "I understand how upset you are about it. I am ready to check everything out and get back to you promptly." During the conversation, repeat the customer's name periodically. People love their names.

Ask the person what he wants done to resolve the complaint. Do not offer the maximum of what you are willing to give at the start because if the customer won't agree with what you offer, you "will be up against the wall." (Again, this is the negotiation approach.) When you and the complainant come to an agreement, repeat what has been agreed upon and ask the person whether he understood everything.

It is important that your company representatives who are at the forefront of contact with clients, customers, suppliers, and others have trained voices and a sense of responsibility for the organization. Don't forget to encourage and reward people who work in the "trenches." They are a good investment in your business.

Ten Commandments of a Successful Business

Should everyone be in business on her own? The desire to own a business is not enough; it requires an analytical mind and pragmatic thinking, energy, and the will to succeed. Not everyone possesses these qualities to a degree to be successful in business. Of course, to work in your own business boosts self-esteem, offers the opportunity to realize your own ideas and independence, and enables you to make more money, among other benefits. It's been observed that people who work for themselves are more confident, are more satisfied with life, and are able to better plan their future. However, in business, there is always a risk of losing money and wasting time. First come the inevitable stress, fear of failure, and possible conflicts in the family. Not every family is willing to risk their savings or to get into debt for the sake of the idea of future earnings. Hopefully, the following "commandments" will help you develop and retain your business for years to come.

1. *Knowledge of your field of business.* Do not go into a business just because someone else is successful in a similar business. Analyze your strengths and weaknesses and compare them to the requirements of the future business. You should be confident in your ability to conduct it, which will give you a head start on competitors. You have to love the field of the business you are going to get in. You should do your due diligence and research before investing your money in a potential business.

2. *Goals and objectives.* Set clear goals that you wish to achieve. J. C. Penney once said: "Give me a clerk from the packaging department who has a goal, and I will give you a man who will go down in history. Give me a man who has no goal, and I will give you a clerk for the packaging department" (as cited in Ziglar, 2004).
3. *Responsibility.* One of the common reasons for of starting a business is the desire to be your "own boss," the desire to implement your ideas and dreams in life, the desire to be in a position of control. However, along with being your own boss comes the associated responsibilities, even though it seems like there is no one to answer to. You have to do everything to make your product or service superior to your competitors'. In failures and blunders, blame no one, neither your subordinates, nor suppliers, nor customers. You get "rewards" if your business is doing well, and you can blame only yourself if it's not.
4. *Dedication and persistence.* It is difficult to count on success in business by devoting a marginal amount of your time and potential output to it by working in spurts and raids. You must be willing to work long hours if necessary. Such situations are very common, especially in start-ups.
5. *Concentration.* Even when you are away from your business, your brain should be constantly open to the perception of your surroundings, in search of the things that can be transferred to your business. Ask your employees to offer any ideas that can improve your business, even ideas from other types of businesses. They are in the trenches. Extracting ideas from the staff and implementing them is beneficial to the business. Encourage and reward your people for their valuable contributions.
6. *Coordination and control.* It is impossible to cover all aspects of the business yourself. Remember, one person can do the work of one person. Search for reliable staff and delegate tasks to them. The ability to efficiently coordinate the efforts of subordinates is an absolutely necessary factor in business. Similarly, the efficient use of equipment, energy, resources, materials, systems, and the like helps reduce the cost of doing business. "A penny saved is a penny earned," goes the American proverb.
7. *Effective communication.* A misunderstanding of conditions described in contracts with suppliers, purchasers, and others can result in large losses. Similarly, instructions and assignments that you give to subordinates must be understood as you intend them to be. It would not hurt to hear from them about how they understand your instructions or assignments and what you expect of them. Communication with customers is as important. Sharing information within the organization is critical; often things are overlooked or consistency is not achieved due to ineffective communication.
8. *Ingenuity.* The business must grow from year to year. A business standing in place will do poorly or may not survive. You have to constantly think about

improving your business. Those might be additional services, related products, or anything else that other similar businesses do not have.

9. *Ethics in conducting a business.* Honesty and cooperation with people and organizations you are in business relationships with are necessary factors for success in business. Every businessperson wants to maintain business relationships with suppliers, customers, and clients for many years. If you manipulate, mislead, and so on, you will find it hard to maintain a good reputation. Your business contacts' satisfaction and their referrals are the best advertising. People talk. Word of mouth is critical and can be a monumental force for good or bad.

10. *Never give up!* Perhaps the most famous example of success through failure is Colonel Sanders, the founder of the Kentucky Fried Chicken restaurant chain. At the age of 62, when many were preparing for retirement, he barely made enough to pay off his bills. He drove from town to town, diner to diner offering owners the use of his chicken recipe in exchange for some small commission for each piece sold. A thousand and eight people looked him directly in the eye and said no. He could have said to himself, "Well I tried" and just walked away, but Colonel Sanders was one stubborn colonel. Finally, person number 1,009 said, "Yes"! Amazing, isn't it? Now Kentucky Fried Chicken restaurants are in every corner of the world. Of course, times change and marketing methods are very different today, but methods are just the tools in achieving goals. The idea is the same: Never give up!.

Chapter 6 in a Few Lines

1. Dr. Peter's Theory of Incompetence should be in the back of the mind of all those who make decisions for promoting an employee to the managerial level or promoting a low-level manager to a higher managerial position.
2. Dr. Chester Karrass's book title *In Business and in Life You Don't Get What You Deserve, You Get What You Negotiate* sounds like good advice.
3. Managers, not employees are in a position to regulate the psychological climate in the work environment. Every manager from the one on the lowest level to the one on the highest level must develop skills to control his or her own stress and to look for ways to diminish stressful factors in the workplace for subordinates.
4. The offered business tips are only a very few that you can use in your work and in communicating with other people. You probably know of some other ones; your friends and colleagues know theirs as well. Share these tips with your colleagues and friends. Use them in your work with people and in your life, and you will experience their value.

References

Cohen, H. (1980). *You Can Negotiate Anything*. New York: Bantam Books.
Ferguson, M. (1980). *The Aquarian Conspiracy: Personal and Social Transformation in the 1980s*. Los Angeles, CA: J. P. Tarcher.
Freeman, G. L. (1948). *The energetics of human behavior*. Ithaca, New York: University Press.
Friedman, M. and Ulmer, D. (1984). *Treating Type A Behavior and Your Heart*. New York: Fawcett Crest Book.
Giblin, L. (1985). *How to Have Confidence and Power in Dealing with People*. Englewood Cliffs, NJ: Prentice-Hall.
Pausch, R. and Zaslow, J. (2008). *The Last Lecture*. New York: Hyperion.
Peter, L. J. and Hull, R. (1969). *The Peter Principle: Why Things Always Go Wrong*. New York: William Morrow and Co., Inc.
Selye, H. (1956). *The Stress of Life*. New York: McGraw-Hill.
Shumkov, G. E. (1913). Anxiety as the dominant emotion in anticipation of the battle. *Military Journal*, Issue 11, 12–21. St. Petersburg, Russia.
Ziglar, Z. (2004). *Great Quotes from Zig Ziglar: 250 Inspiring Quotes from the Master Motivator and Friends*. New York: Gramercy Books.

7

YOUR IMAGE IS IN YOUR HANDS

You optimistically consider yourself an expert in your industry and know how to get along with people; that is, you consider yourself a good manager. Congratulations! However, is it enough to implement your knowledge and skills in leading your people in a satisfactory and successful professional life? "But what else?" is the question. The "else" is that a certain level of mental and physical state is needed to implement your knowledge and skills. Your subordinates want to see their manager as energetic, confident, and in a good spirit.

Factors to Pay Attention To

Stereotypes

The perception of humans by humans is a big topic in social psychology. We will briefly consider only one aspect—stereotypes. In the late 1960s, psychologists of Leningrad University (now St. Petersburg University, Russia) conducted a simple but useful experiment on stereotypes. Experimenters entered classrooms with another man and asked students to determine his profession. The man entered different classrooms wearing different attire. In the first one, he walked in dressed up in plain working clothes, in the second, dressed casually, and in the third wearing a suit and a tie. As the man was changing into more "intellectual" clothing before entering the next classroom, the percentage of "intellectual" occupations given by students grew rapidly.

In our daily lives, when meeting people for the first time, we perceive them on the basis of stereotypes that exist in our mind based on our life experience. Stereotyping involves classifying people into groups, and based on the characteristics of the group into which they have been classified, we make inferences about them. We make judgments about people's personalities based on our first impression, which has a crucial influence on our fixing of a certain stereotype. The first impression about a person is usually so firm that it may change only upon the critical assessment of the person's actions. Russians say, "Welcoming by the appearance, saying good-bye by the intellect."

Our society is changing and so are the stereotypes, but nevertheless people still rely on stereotypes in their everyday lives. They are still quite useful for the purposes of interaction with other people. Stereotypes contain sufficient practical information relating to the person to whom they are applied. And as long as they are useful, one can create a certain image of himself in the eyes of others, especially at the first meeting. It can be achieved not only by controlling attire but also by emphasizing some external factors like gait, handshake, manner of speaking, and so on. In this connection, let's consider some physical parameters and other external factors that you can control in order to create the desired image in the eyes of others.

The Factors

Your posture. Correct posture is expressed as follows: straight torso, elevated chin, slightly opened deployed shoulders, clear step, discreet smile, and smooth breathing. All of this will create an image of a confident person. By following these rules, you will feel taller, your voice will sound more confident, and you will be able to establish eye contact with people. When you assume an expansive, powerful position, you will feel more powerful and in more control. Incorrect posture may cause the opposite; you will seem vulnerable in the eyes of your opponents. Similarly, you have to control your posture when sitting; it should be as confident as your posture while walking and standing. Do not sit deep on the couch or on an armchair so that your knees are near your chin because doing that will "sit" you at a disadvantage in a direct and figurative sense. If the couch or armchair is your only choice, then sit on the edge of it and sit straight as though someone is pulling you up.

The handshake and the voice. In the business world, the handshake is one of the signs of amicable relations. Shake hands not only when you are being introduced, but when you say goodbye, when you congratulate people, and so on. The handshake should be short and active, while you look the person in the eye. A brief energetic full hand handshake is associated with confidence.

The pace of speech is very important. If you speak fast, it might make an impression that you are nervous; if slow, it can be understood as uncertainty and lack of energy. Control yourself in speaking clearly, at a reasonable pace, with normal volume. Some people, when talking on the phone, like to do it standing up; standing gives them more confidence. Before beginning the call, wake up your interest, enthusiasm, and confidence. If the person to whom you are calling is not there, leave a clear message. Similarly, the greeting in your voice mailbox should be recorded with a confident energetic voice.

Eye contact and distance. It is no revelation to say that it is proper to look at the person you are talking with. However, this commonsense factor is not always seen in reality. By looking directly at the person, you will think more clearly and will be able to better deliver your thoughts. Similarly, by watching the other person's reaction to what you are saying, you can adjust the content of what you are trying to convey.

Regarding the distance between you and another person during a conversation, there are no specific numerical parameters on that. The only thing worth noting is that in different cultures, the distance between people during conversations varies. Generally speaking, everyone has some sort of personal space, the invasion of which may cause a negative reaction. Sometimes people tend to stand too close to a person, who then has to step back from the speaker. Try not to forget this, and keep a reasonable distance, especially if you are in a culture different from yours.

The Language That No One Studies But Everyone Speaks

It's body language, of course, the language of facial expressions and gestures, posture and manners, and the like. Body language is a nonverbal method of communication whose content can be interpreted by others. Nonverbal communication is very useful, but its interpretation is subjective and brings the possibility of error. All people, to a greater or lesser extent, speak the language of facial expressions and gestures.

Unlike verbal language, nonverbal language has one unique quality: internationalism. Someone said, "Everyone smiles in the same language." Historically, a nonverbal way to communicate appeared much earlier than the verbal did. Most basic human emotions—joy, anger, fear, surprise, and some others—manifest themselves in similar ways in different countries. However, though the basic human emotions are universal, the meanings of some body language gestures in different cultures are different. When preparing to travel abroad, especially for a business trip, it's worth familiarizing yourself with the meaning of the body language in the country you are going to visit. For example, in Japan when people nod while you are speaking, it does not necessarily mean that they understand and agree. The following real case was described in the San Francisco Russian newspaper *The View* (2003) can serve as an illustration:

> An unusual process took place years ago in a court in Berlin. A driver in a passing vehicle showed a policeman a hand gesture—the thumb and index fingers touching each other in a shape of a ring. In different cultures this gesture is interpreted in different ways, either as an OK, which is an admiration or delight, or as a serious offense—"you are a jerk in the eyes of humanity." The police officer filed a lawsuit against the driver insisting that it was an assault. The judge, after rummaging through the suitable literature

and consulting with psychologists, concluded that in Germany both meanings of the signal are acceptable. The driver was acquitted.

Through different movements of our body, face, and eyes, we share information about our true feelings and intentions, which may or may not coincide with what we are trying to convey by talking. Nonverbal behavior is more difficult for people to control because it is almost unconscious; therefore, their facial expressions and gestures are less likely to pose deception. Precisely these components of behavior, in contrast to verbal language, convey an emotional state, mood shades, and so forth. All of these, especially facial expression, give more accurate information about what other people are trying to convey than carefully selected words. Body language can open another person's thoughts with more certainty. The results of numerous studies confirmed that the verbal component of a face-to-face dialogue is about 35%, while the nonverbal component is about 65%. Thus, the language of gestures and facial expressions can serve as a tool for analyzing the extent to which verbal information coincides with nonverbal. Not accidentally, specialists in reading body language are present at trials watching for the slightest changes in facial expression, posture, and other nonverbal behavioral components of the accused and others in the courtroom.

For a better understanding of body language, start with yourself. Try to observe and analyze your body language in different emotional states. Ask yourself these questions: What does my body project to others? Where do I keep my hands? Are my fingers locked? Where are my eyes directed? Is my chin up or down? Do I keep my head straight, or is it tilted sideways? And so on. Learn how to control the movements of your own body with the purpose of sending only those signals that you want to send. Watch the gestures and facial expressions of others, and try to read what they really want to say. Learn how to connect information that other people are trying to convey verbally simultaneously with "the words" of their body movements.

To demonstrate such qualities as confidence, courage, dedication, and other moral and volitional qualities, try to practice the following: control your posture, don't look down when walking or chatting with others; do not extend a "weak" hand for a handshake; squeeze the hand of another person with a brief energetic handshake, accompanied with eye contact.

A Moving Target Is Harder to Hit

"Fashionable" Diseases

The incredible technological progress of the last two centuries has brought considerable relief to humans in terms of the reduction of physical effort in the workplace. However, precisely the same technological progress was and is the main cause of many "fashionable" diseases of our time. Diseases of the cardiovascular system, back problems, the deterioration of hands, poor vision, and others—all are a by-product of technological progress. Modern, technologically advanced tools, which practically do not require an application of physical efforts, motor vehicles, industrial automation and computerization, the enhancement of living conditions, and the like have caused a massive lack of physical activity, with all the ensuing consequences. We must not forget that our forefathers for many millennia walked, ran, were active with their hands using primitive tools, and so on. And now, we, the inheritors of their genes where the constant movement is coded, "abruptly stopped and sat down."

The typical position of most people during the day is sitting. People sit at work, in transport, at the dining table, in front of the computer and TV, and elsewhere. What this means is that most muscle groups are not active, which leads to poor blood circulation and causes premature fatigue. Not accidentally, sitting is accused of all the "sins." Sitting does no good for the body; it may even diminish the good of exercising. So anything that gets you up from the sitting position, even briefly, is a good thing. If you do sit at work, then sit straight. Posture matters for your health. Slouching indicates low muscle tone, which may be the result of a lack of physical activity. Slouch sitting compresses your core and crowds the organs (liver, stomach, pancreas, etc.) so that the blood flow through these organs is not going the way it should, thus interfering with their optimal functioning. When walking or sitting, keep your head level and pretend a string is pulling your head upward, keep your shoulder blades back and down, and tuck in your stomach.

With the progress of computer technology, the situation with hands has worsened too. Those who perform a large volume of monotonous work on computers suffer the most. Injuries caused by intensive work on computers, the so-called "cumulative injuries", are very hard to treat. Piano performers knew about such traumas long before the computer era. The percentage of diseases of back and hands grew within the last few decades, and this trend continues.

Our Muscles

The cause of so-called "muscle hunger" is due to the lack of physical activity. The only way out of physical inactivity is physical activity. The Russian folk saying "In a healthy body there is a healthy spirit!" is of direct relevance to any person who manages other people's activity. A physically fit manager increases her self-esteem and contributes to a more effective implementation of knowledge and skills. The manager's vivacity, good mood, and taut appearance cause positive emotions within subordinates. There is only one way to quench muscle hunger—through systematic physical activity. The great medieval doctor Avicenna expressed figuratively that a person who moderately and consistently exercises needs no treatment. The purpose of exercise is to make the heart work more actively. As a result, the capillaries that penetrate throughout all the organs of the body get more blood, thus providing them with the necessary "food" and helping the body be rid of unwanted waste. A faster heart rate also activates breathing. Breathing becomes deeper, helping to remove carbon dioxide from the deepest parts of the lungs.

There are more than 600 muscles in the human body. Muscle weight accounts for about 40% of total body weight. How many of them are functioning during the normal working hours? Optimistically, less than half, and not in a very active way. This means that the muscles get decrepit. Hardly anyone would object that it is bad for the functioning of the human body and organisms as a whole. Developed muscles are not only pleasant aesthetically, but most importantly they help maintain good posture, and that, in turn, keeps the internal organs in the correct position, contributing to their normal functioning. Poor posture distorts the chest, makes it difficult for the lungs, and causes additional pressure on organs and tissues in the chest and abdomen. Physical activity, particularly systematic physical exercise, is the most effective stress management technique. Exercise can boost brain power because it is strongly linked to mental sharpness. Hence, it is clear that it is important to exercise and to keep muscles in constant tone.

Russian physiologist Ivan Pavlov called the state experienced by people who exercise regularly "muscle joy." A surprising property of the muscles is not limited to the examples of phenomenal strength and endurance. Humans, by arbitrarily changing muscle tone, can influence mood and bring on a state of relaxation or, vice versa, the state of cheerfulness, the readiness to act, can influence recovery performance after a hard day. Working muscles send impulses to the brain, stimulate the nervous system, increase its efficiency, and improve emotional state. Muscle activity is the integral result of the mental and emotional state of humans. If a person does not move enough, the complex of emotional stress may form in the mind, requiring emotional discharge. Movement is what serves as the mechanism of emotional discharge.

The Sechenov Phenomenon

It is well-known that, in order to function effectively, people need to have a periodic complete rest. A good night's sleep is the best rest; it restores energy. However, other forms of rest are also necessary for the normal functioning of the organism. The activity of our nervous system is based on the principle of alternating the *excitation* and *inhibition* processes. That is, as some cerebral nerve centers are in the state of excitation, others are in the state of inhibition at the same time. Namely, this fact, well-known in physiological science, led famous Russian physiologist Ivan Sechenov to an experiment that he conducted in 1901.

With the use of a device of his own design called an ergograph, he conducted two series of experiments. In the first series, a subject lifted a load with his finger over a small pulley until completely exhausted. After that, the subject had a period of rest until a full recovery. It took him 10 minutes. Then the subject repeated the same task with the same finger. In the second series, instead of the passive rest after lifting the load, the subject performed the same task with his finger of the other hand. The results of the experiment surprised Sechenov. The subject needed only two and a half minutes for a full recovery after the "active rest," that is, after performing the task with the "second" finger. In other words, the fatigued "first" hand was capable of much greater exertion after the work done by the "second" hand than it had been after the first period of rest. This led Sechenov to the conclusion that the leading role in the process of fatigue relaxation belongs to the nervous system. The experiment has gone down in the history of physiological science as the Sechenov phenomenon and is known as the basis for active rest. Later on, the results of Sechenov's experiment were interpreted broadly as "the best rest is a change of activity." It accelerates the recovery of the "tired" nerve centers and muscles and restores the normal functioning of the organism more rapidly. It serves as the physiological basis of the active rest benefits.

Alternating work activity with physical activity or house chores or reading, or switching the content of reading from serious to fiction, or switching one kind of exercise to a different kind, and so on are all good and simple ways to use our mind and body more efficiently. If you feel that the work process does not flow so effectively, it means that the nerve centers of the brain that are responsible for the given activity are in the stage of fatigue. In such cases, give them some rest by putting them into the inhibition state. According to Sechenov, the best way to do this is to bring other nerve centers of the brain into the state of excitation; that is, put them "to work." As a result, those "tired" nerve centers will recover faster. In other words, it is desirable to switch the activity within your work responsibilities given that the specifics of the work allow you to do so. This method helps to maintain the optimum efficiency of work activity during the working day. Short breaks at the workplace every couple of hours for 2–3 minutes to perform some exercises contribute to the removal of the developing fatigue by activating the ventilation in the lower lobes of the lungs, thus relieving the tension of the tired body, mainly the back, neck, and eyes.

Fatigue

Fatigue is a normal physiological condition of a temporary decrease of an organ or organism's working capacity, resulting from prolonged or strenuous activity, which manifests itself in decreased performance. Fatigue is a useful human reaction to any activity. The biological role of fatigue is the timely protection of the body from exhaustion. Inhibition of the nervous system is a universal mechanism that protects the nervous system and, through it, protects all organs and tissues from starvation, which may even result in the body losing its vitality. If a person avoids getting tired, it not only prevents the person from developing endurance, which is closely connected with the volitional qualities, but may even bring some harm.

Fatigue manifests itself in different forms: physical, mental, or emotional. Different forms of fatigue require different forms of rest. Sometimes a deterioration of one's mood, which is quite changeable, is merely due to the fatigue produced by routine or monotonous work, and it suffices to change it in order to get back to a normal condition and to keep the nervous system in check. For example, if a person gets tired from physical work, reading can be a useful form of active rest. If it is mental fatigue, a sports game could be a good form of rest. If it is emotional exhaustion, prolonged low-intensity physical activity, such as a long walk, is useful for restoring the normal condition of the organism.

We spend up to 70% of our waking hours at work. Therefore, it's important to do whatever is possible to make your workplace comfortable in order to maintain the maximum level of efficiency. In particular, this mainly applies to those who sit at work most of the day. No athlete will compete in uncomfortable or awkward sportswear or shoes because she wants to achieve maximum results. But many "office athletes" neglect to take care of these things at the workplace, and as a result it negatively affects the state of the organism and performance.

Movement Is Life

Bodily movement is a normal state of any organism, including the human body. The human body is not made for sitting! Modern humans in civilized countries have become hostages of sitting. Dr. James Levine at the Mayo Clinic, who coined the phrase "Sitting is the new smoking," states that "we are sitting ourselves to death." Everyone is able to commit to the required minimum amount of time for regular physical activity. Even 30–40 minutes of physical activity during the day can be a minimally sufficient amount of physical "food" for the body. The most accessible and harmless form of exercise is walking. Jogging is also healthy; however, lengthy jogging can potentially cause back and knee problems. The reason is that, in running, the feet repetitively hit the ground. The body weight at that moment increases, and such repeated blows of feet on the ground cause micro tremors of the body. And that cannot be good for the runners' knee joints. Walking, particularly brisk walking, can provide the same benefits to health as jogging but without the risk of such potential injuries. Active walking can improve blood circulation; prevent diseases of the cardiovascular system; provide toning for leg muscles; maintain healthy and strong bones; activate the respiratory system; reduce symptoms of stress, depression, slackness; and help control weight due to a more intensive metabolism.

Physiologists call walking the "second heart" because rhythmically straining muscles squeeze the veins and push the blood up toward the heart, thus helping the heart to work. When a person is in a sitting position for a prolonged time, blood circulation becomes passive; it accumulates in the abdominal area and in hips and legs. That makes the heart work harder in order to deliver the needed amount of oxygen to all the cells of the body. Feasible daily physical activity improves the body's resistance to diseases, helps fight fatigue, stimulates brain activity, and has a positive effect on the ability to work. By including any kind of exercise or other physical activity in your weekly schedule, you do yourself good. A trained heart uses less oxygen, thus creating a safety margin in case of a heart attack.

Some people consider themselves so busy that they can't even find the minimal time for walking or other exercises. An American proverb states, "If there is a will, there is a way." If you are really so busy and cannot find time to do some minimum physical activity before or after work, try these little "tricks." If you commute to work by public transportation, walk one or two stops to your work. If you drive to work, park your car a few blocks away from work; "ignore" elevators, use stairs instead. Take the longest path to get a cup of coffee or to use a toilet, do some walking before returning to your workplace. At every opportunity, move within the building where you work; use a part of the lunch break to go outside and walk. Change your body position regularly; occasionally walk around the room. Get up from the chair not by leaning forward but by pushing yourself up with your arms. Stand up while talking on the phone, bend forward and backward, left and right; put one knee on the chair while talking.

In addition to these activities, stretching exercises are easy to do, and you need no exercise equipment or a gym. Your desktop, the back of your desk chair, the doorway of your office is all that you need. Stretching is called a cure for people whose work obliges them to sit for long hours. Stretching helps relax the strained muscles from prolonged sitting and prevents problems with the back and hands. Stretching in a standing position improves blood circulation, especially in the legs and abdominal area; it also gives some rest for a stiff back and neck. These exercises will help to remove the accumulated tension, clear the mind, and renew creative ability.

Doing all these simple physical activities during the working day may feel strange at first but eventually will become a habit and will do real good. By using these and other similar "tricks," even with an incredible workload, you will give your body the minimum required physical activity during the working day. You will have more energy and feel better after work. Remember, it's harder for heart diseases to hit a "moving target"!

Chapter 7 in a Few Lines

1. Create your image as you want it to be in the eyes of others. Monitor your posture, gait, rhythm, and volume of voice; in conversations, always look at the other person and give a vigorous handshake.
2. Watch your nonverbal signals and learn to "read" the body language of others.
3. A change of activities is the best way to maintain the normal functioning of the organism.
4. Strive to find any opportunity to give your body at least the minimum amount of physical activity of 30–40 minutes a day 3–4 times a week.
5. A useful lesson that managers can learn from athletes is not to give up after unsuccessful competitions. They do not stop training but train harder to win the next one. The development of such a quality is important for effective management.

Reference

What Body Language Tells Us About (July 5–11, 2003). *The View*, San Francisco.

8

LEARN TO CONTROL YOURSELF

51 Illustrated Psychological Recommendations for Optimizing Manager–Employee Relations

In management, just as in parenting, there are no minor things. Every word you say, every glance you project, and every gesture you make are being fixed in the minds of subordinates and thus creating a definite opinion about you. The offered recommendations in no way cover all possible situations that arise in the multifaceted activities of managing. But hopefully they will do their part in helping you to establish good relationships with subordinates and in leading them in a successful and satisfactory professional life.

1. Subordinates expect you to lead. They are aware that they will be held accountable for poor performance. The only thing they are not prepared for is a manager who does not know what he wants and does not notice their poor performance.

2. Decisiveness and courage are necessary qualities for managers. The manager who avoids issues and shows a passive attitude loses credibility and demonstrates the inability to manage.

3. Combine your own knowledge with the ability to mobilize the knowledge of those who you manage.

4. One person can do the work of one person. Transferring parts of your authority to subordinates is the way to stimulate them and to increase productivity. Delegate!

5. The manager is responsible for the functioning of the team during her absence. You must train your subordinates so that at least one of them will be able to replace you in your absence so that your team will continue to operate effectively.

6. Do not confine yourself to the narrow frame of your technical expertise. Your job is to manage. Use your subordinates' valuable qualities to enhance productivity without the administrative pressure.

7. If what your subordinates are doing is fundamentally at odds with your opinion, give them maximum freedom of action. You will be pleasantly surprised at what interesting ideas and solutions they can offer.

8. Advising subordinates does not mean thinking for them. Encourage them to find their own solutions for the issues with which they came to you. Ask how they are going to do it, but be prepared to answer their questions.

9. Learn not only how to resolve various problems but to be alert about possibly undesirable situations. It will give you an opportunity to take appropriate actions in advance.

10. Time has material value; do not waste it. Plan your working day carefully and follow the schedule. The effective use of time is one of the ways to enhance productivity.

11. Meetings should be strictly regulated in time. Involve in meetings only those who are able to actively discuss emerging issues and who are competent in them.

12. It is always possible to use time more efficiently. During the commute or waiting for the train, review your notes, check e-mails, plan your day, and get other quick things done.

13. Do not obstruct your memory when it is not necessary. Make notes of your fleeting thoughts, about upcoming business affairs, and the like. It will help to keep some minor everyday things under control.

14. The manager who depicts himself as a know-it-all negatively impacts the flow of the team activity with all its undesirable consequences. It most likely will lead to subordinates' dissatisfaction with working under such a manager.

15. Don't be afraid to say, "I don't know" or "I made a mistake." If you were wrong, have the courage to admit it. Remember, none of your slipups will go unnoticed.

16. Never break a promise. And do not make a promise if you are not sure that you can perform. You can deceive others once or twice but lose their trust forever.

IF YOU ARE NOT SURE – DO NOT PROMISE

17. Do not show haste in making serious decisions. People will understand if you say, "I need some time to think about it. Can it wait until tomorrow?"

18. Never make subordinates do work that they are not good at. Strive to give each of them the tasks that best match their abilities and aptitudes.

19. Tasks and assignments may be stressful but must be realistic. Think carefully about whether it can be done on time. Check the subordinate's current work load before giving him a new assignment.

20. Never hide information, either good or bad, from your subordinates. Keep them informed about the real state of affairs. An environment of rumors and speculations is not a desirable psychological atmosphere in the workplace.

21. Constantly study your subordinates. Nobody is perfect, but everyone is good at something. Have tolerance for their weaknesses as long as they do not interfere with work. Use their strengths and you will not notice their weaknesses.

22. People are filled with thoughts and ideas. They want them to be considered and implemented. Consult with your subordinates, and let them feel importance.

23. Two things motivate people the most: achievements and the acknowledgment of achievements by superiors. Do not miss any opportunity to let your subordinates know how important they are to the company.

24. Share the limelight with your subordinates. Nothing inspires people more than the recognition of their participation in the team's success. Nothing discourages them more than the boss taking all the credit.

25. Be aware of the presence of informal leaders in your production unit. When necessary, try to influence the group through them.

26. Do not give special treatment to some of the team members. Doing so annoys and offends others and creates an unhealthy atmosphere.

27. Be respectful of people's opinions even if you don't agree with them. If a subordinate suggests something that cannot be accepted, explain why. To reject a suggestion without giving a reason creates a false impression about you.

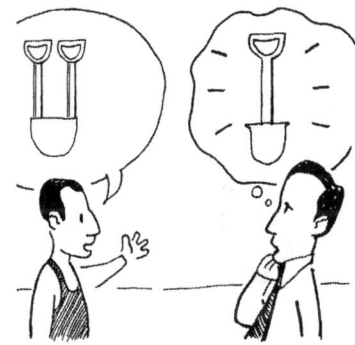

28. Be kind to people, it helps to establish an atmosphere of trust and acceptance. When arriving to work, greet people enthusiastically. People in a good mood perform better.

29. Never criticize subordinates in the presence of others. It can cause the feeling of hatred toward you. Be generous if the subordinate makes a minor error.

30. Don't lose self-control and try to keep calm at all times. Demonstrate enthusiasm even if you don't feel like it.

31. Rudeness is a sign of weakness, not strength. Demands should never be expressed rudely. If you made a rude or tasteless comment, apologize. It will not reduce your credibility but rather increase it.

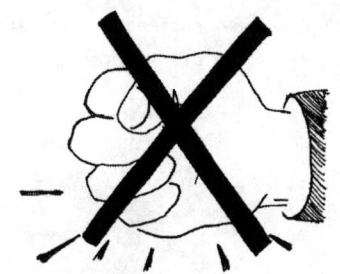

32. You should never express your dissatisfaction in a state of anger. It will be very difficult to correct the relationships. The frequent use of punishment is evidence of an improper way of dealing with subordinates.

33. Never make comments at work like, "I am bored" or "I am tired." Never sit around subordinates doing nothing; it lowers your credibility.

34. A silent worker is a mystery and difficult to manage. Try to engage him in a conversation and, if needed, offer your assistance.

35. When a subordinate comes to complain, let her "let off some steam" to relieve her mental stress. After that, a good portion of the complaint will resolve itself.

36. If in an effort to do something useful, a subordinate makes a mistake, do not harshly criticize him. The criticism may discourage him from taking the initiative in the future. In criticism, consider not only the circumstances but the individual's personality features.

37. Each employee must report to only one superior from whom she receives orders.

38. When a new employee arrives to work, congratulate him. Inform him how important his work is in the overall affairs of the organization. Describe the requirements and point out the possible difficulties associated with the work.

39. Respect calls for mutual respect. If you do not respect your subordinates, they will not respect you. In such a case, you will have only formal power.

40. Do not expect subordinates to show friendliness and affability at first. Be the first one to show it. Even if they don't immediately respond to it, your friendliness will prevail eventually.

41. Congratulate your subordinates on their landmark dates and try to do it in person. It helps to build positive relationships and works as a reinforcement for better performance.

42. Do not burn bridges. You will be amazed how often in business you will need to cross these bridges again.

43. Do business with those who do business with you. Remember the names of people with whom you are in business contact. Do not assume that they remember your name even if you've met before.

44. Do not think of yourself as infallible. Analyze your behavior and work methods. Objectively assess your weak qualities and try to work on them. Constantly look for ways to improve your work.

45. Irritability and restlessness are undesirable characteristics for managers. Keep such manifestations of your behavior under control; otherwise management will be a constant stress for you and for your subordinates. If you often get annoyed and experience anxiety, leave managerial work.

46. Humor has a positive effect on people. Demonstrate a sense of humor and appreciate it in others. Many situations may be improved more by an appropriate joke than by a serious attitude.

47. Don't miss an opportunity to conduct nonbusiness events, such as team celebrations, country trips, group visits, and the like. It improves relationships and motivates people to work together.

48. Do not use off-duty events to discuss business matters. Show subordinates that you are a human too. Let them see that you are their boss only at work.

49. Create the image you want to have in the eyes of others. Have an active handshake and look the person in the eye during conversation. Monitor your posture and body language.

50. You don't have to be doing something all the time: supervising, organizing, coordinating, and so on. Dedicate some of your time just for thinking.

51. Don't lose courage under any circumstances. Conversely, when faced with difficulties, show more energy and achieve victory. Never give up!

Chapter 8 in a Few Lines

> Even in the daily affairs of managing a business or a group of workers—in leadership of any kind—no one is truly worthy of such responsibility unless he has first learned self-control. This is the first essential in the application of the innate ability with which he is equipped.
>
> Ernest Holmes, American writer and spiritual leader

★ ★ ★

We hope that, after reading this book, you will be imbued by the need to take the human element into account in the process of management. It will enable you to create a positive psychological environment in your production unit. In turn, it will help maximize your subordinates' potential and achieve success.

You Can Be Effective in Management!

INDEX

7 Habits of Highly Effective People, The (Covey) 95
13 Fatal Errors Managers Make and How You Can Avoid Them (Brown) 85, 102
60 Minutes (television) 98
1501 Ways to Reward Employees (Nelson) 94

Abilene paradox 67–8
abilities *see* human abilities
activity *see* individual style of activity
activity theory: activity as mediator 13–14; human mind development 13–16; personality principal 14–15; self-regulation of activity 15–16
adaptation: concept of 66–7; forms of 67–9; professional 69–71; psychological security 71–2; *see also* groups
advice *see* business tips
Aircraft Noise Insulation Project 85, 87
American Beauty (movie) 58
American Bureau of Labor Statistic 82
analyzers: nervous system 21–3
Aristotle 37, 59
Ash, Mary Kay 101
Ashby, William Ross 65, 73n4

Baryshnikov, Mikhail 32
Becoming a Manager: Mastery of a New Identity (Hill) 80
Behaviorism 14–15
Bennis, Warren 35, 87

Big Five personality traits 23
Blanchard, Ken 77
body language 132–3
body movement 137–8
Bonaparte, Napoleon 20
bosses: delegating power 78–80; desire for good 82–90; handling subordinates 86–8; management styles 82–4; motivating employees 88–90, 146; not competing with subordinates 84–6, 144; power of words 90–4; sharing limelight with employees 89–90, 146; stress in work of managers 118–19; valuing subordinates 88–90; working relationships 91–2; *see also* management
Brown, Steven 85, 102
business tips: business letters 122–3; dealing with angry customers 125–6; do it now! 120; handling criticism 123–5; manager-employee relations 140–53; partnership advice 120–1; presentation details 121–2; ten commandments for successful business 126–8

Cerebral Mechanism of Behavior symposium 14
Challenger (shuttle) accident 68
character 28; characterizing 25–6; "inconvenient" 27; traits of 26–7
choleric temperament 18, 20, 23, 28
Chrysler Corporation 93, 98
Cohen, Herb 110

collaborators: communication 100, 101
communication: barriers 98–100; business letters 122–3; competence 97; dealing with angry customers 125–6; as human ability 94–5; manager-employee 145; nonverbal and verbal signals 97; nonverbal language 132–3; personality types 100–1; striving for clear 95–8; for successful business 127
Communist Party 39
compatibility: groups 59–66; teamwork 76–8
concentration: in business 127
conditional reflexes: signal system 21, 28
conformity 67–8
Cooley, Charles 53
Cooper, Chris 58
Corday, Barbara 87
Covey, Stephen 95
criticism: handling 123–5; of subordinates 147, 148, 149
Crusoe, Robinson 94
cumulative injuries 134
customers: dealing with angry 125–6

Darwin, Charles 22, 34
da Vinci, Leonardo 37
delegation 78–80, 141
De Niro, Robert 89
Dewey, John 88
diseases: "fashionable" 134
dizygotic twins 34

Edison, Thomas 32
Einstein, Albert 37, 38, 39
Emotional Intelligence (Goleman) 40
Employee Motivation Movement 2
employees: bosses not competing with 84–6; bosses valuing 88–90; delegating power to 78–80; informal leaders 56, 80–2; managers handling 86–8; managers motivating 88–90, 146; managers sharing limelight with 89–90, 146; optimizing manager-employee relations 140–53; positive reinforcement 89; professional adaptation 69–71; *see also* bosses
engineering psychology 5, 8–10
EQ (emotional quotient) 40
ergonomics 5, 8–10; human factors 10
ethics 128
exercise: physical activity 134–5
extraversion 23–5, 28

eye contact 132
Eysenck, Hans 23

Facebook 70
fatigue 136–7
Federal Aviation Administration (FAA) 9
feral children 50
Ferguson, Marilyn 121
Fernández-Aráoz, Claudio 41
followers: communication 100, 101
formal groups 54–7
Franklin, Benjamin 90
Freud, Sigmund 110
Friedman, Meyer 117

Galton, Sir Francis 34
general adaptation syndrome (GAS) 116
genetics 16; twin study method 34–5
genius: human abilities 37
Gilbreth, Frank 3
Gilbreth, Lillian 3
Gogol, Nikolai 20, 38
Golden Rule 76
Goleman, Daniel 35, 40
Gorbov, Feodor 65
Great Depression 40
group dynamics 52, 73n1
groups: adaptation concept 66–7; compatibility factor 59–66; environment for human development 49–50; feelings in 61–2; formal 54–7; forms of adaptation 67–9; incompatibility in 61–2; informal 54–7; interconnected and noninterconnected activity 62–4; measuring interpersonal relationships 64–6; not arithmetic sum of individuals 59–62; primary social 53–4; professional adaptation 69–71; psychological security 71–2; reference 54; role conflicts 58–9; secondary social 53–4; small social 52–3; social facilitation 50–2; social roles of 57–9; teamwork 60
Gurevich, K.M. 41–2
gymnasts: individual style 44; Kerri Strug 51; social facilitation 51–2

handshake 131
Harwood Manufacturing Corporation 69
Hathaway, Anne 89
Heller, Robert 80
Heraclitus 25
Hi Five! The Magic of Working Together (Blanchard) 77

Hill, Linda 80
Hippocrates 18, 19, 20
Holmes, Ernest 40, 153
homeostasis 66, 116
homeostat: group compatibility 65–6
homozygote twins 17
human abilities: abilities and skills 37–8; base of abilities 36; communication as 94–5; general and special 36–7; genius 37; IQ question 39–41; knowledge and intelligence 38–9; professional suitability and reliability 41–2; talent 37
human factors 1, 11; ergonomics 10
human mind: activity theory on development of 13–16
Human Relations Movement 3–4
humans: body movement 137–8; creating your image 130–8, 152; "fashionable" diseases 134; fatigue 136–7; fields studying activity of 5–6; genetics 16; impact of technological progress 4–5; personality features 16–17; physical activity 134–5; social environment for development 49–50; technology and 6–7; tools and 6; *see also* image, creating your

Iacocca, Lee 93
image, creating your 130–8, 152; body language 132–3; body movement 137–8; distance between people 132; eye contact 132; "fashionable" diseases 134; fatigue 136–7; handshake 131; movement 137–8; muscle hunger 134–5; nonverbal language 132–3; pace of speech 131; posture 131; Sechenov's phenomenon 135–6; stereotypes 130–1
In Business and in Life You Don't Get What You Deserve, You Get What You Negotiate (Karrass) 115, 128
incompetence 105–9; being aware 106; *see also* theory of incompetence
individualists: communication 100, 101
individual style of activity 42; concept of 43; gymnasts 44; self-regulation as basis for 43–4; study on 45–6
industrial/organizational psychology 5, 7–8
Industrial Revolution 2, 7
informal groups 54–7
informal leaders 56, 80–2, 146
ingenuity: in business 127–8
intelligence: "bad student" phenomenon 39; IQ question 39–41; knowledge and 38–9, 46
Intern, The (movie) 88
internationalism 132
interpersonal relationships: measurement of 64–6
introversion 23–5, 28

J.C. Penney 113
Johansen, Frederick 63
Johnson, Walter 124
Jones, Jim 54

Kaczynski, Ted 94
Karrass, Chester 115, 128
Kentucky Fried Chicken 128
knowledge: combining 141; and intelligence 38–9, 46

language: business letters 122–3; communication of 95
language barrier 98–9
Lao-Tze 78
Last Lecture, The: Really Achieving Your Childhood Dreams (Pausch) 125
leaders: communication 100
Levine, James 137
Lincoln, Abraham 27
listeners: categories of 102–3; managers as 101–3
Loehr, Jim 26, 29n3
logical barriers 99–100

Makarenko, Anton 57
management: becoming a manager 80–2; communication in 75, 94–101; delegating power 78–80; desire for good bosses 82–90; informal leaders 56, 80–2, 146; as a job 74–82; listening in 101–3; managing people 74–5; Peter Principle 106–8; power of words 90–4; promotion to 80–2; psychology of 3; rewards and sanctions 92–4, 146; stress in work of managers 118–19; styles 82–4; teamwork 76–8; theory of incompetence 106–9; *see also* bosses; business tips; negotiation
manager-employee relations: recommendations for 140–53
Mandelshtam, Osip 38
Marchionne, Sergio 98
Marischuk, V. L. 33

Marshal Kutuzov 20
Mary Kay on People Management (Ash) 101
Mayo, Elton 3–4
melancholic temperament 18, 19, 20, 23, 28
Mills, Wanda 119
monozygotic (identical) twins 26, 34
Moreno, Jacob 64–5
muscle hunger 134–5

Nansen, Fridtjof 63, 73n3
nature *vs* nurture 31–6; debate on 31–3; negative impact on human health 33–4; rationale for debate 35–6; twin study method on debate 34–5
negotiation 109–15; dealing with angry customers 125–6; practicing skills 114–15; striving for win-win situation 112–14; techniques for 110–12
Nelson, Bob 93–4
nervous system: analyzers 21–3; balance of excitation and inhibition 22; extraversion-introversion 23–5; features of 20–1; mobility of 22; neuroticism-stability 23–5; sensitivity 22
neuroticism 23–5, 28
nonverbal language 132–3
Now, Discover Your Strength (Buckingham and Clifton) 32

operant conditioning 14
Owen, Robert 2, 12n1

partnership advice 120–1
Pausch, Randy 125
Pavlov, Ivan 20, 95, 135
Penney, J.C. 113, 127
People's Temple 54
persistence: in business 127, 128
personality: acquired features of 16–17; communicative types of 100–1; nature *vs* nurture 31–6; social influence 50–2, 72; uniqueness of 17
personality principal 14–15
personal space 132
Peter Principle, The (Peter and Hull) 106, 128
Peter the Great (Tsar) 20
phlegmatic temperament 18, 19–20, 23, 28
phonetic barrier 99
physical activity: exercise 134–5; movement 137–8; Sechenov's phenomenon 135–6

physiological incompatibility 61
Plato 122
Plisetskaya, Maya 33
positive reinforcement 89, 150
posture 131
power: management delegating 78–80, 141; social adaptation 68; of words 90–4, 148–50
PQ (personality quotient) 40
prelaunch fever 116
presentations: attending to details in 121–2
primary groups 53–4
Principals of Scientific Management, The (Taylor) 2
procrastination: avoiding 120
professional activity 46; reliability 41–2; suitability 41–2
professional adaptation 69–71; psychological security and 71–2
psychic tension 115
psychological compatibility 63, 72
psychological incompatibility 62
psychological security: groups 71–2
psychology of isolation 50–1
Psychology of Management, The (Gilbreth) 3

Raikin, Arkady 76
reference group 54
reliability: professional activity 41–2
responsibility: in business 127
Revizor (Gogol) 20, 38
rewards: workplace 92–4
role conflicts: groups 58–9
Rubinstein, Sergey 14–15
Russell, Bertrand 86
Russian Civil War of 1918–1920 57
Russian Revolution of 1917 57
Russo-Japanese War of 1904–1905 115
Ryan, Leo 54

sanctions: workplace 92–4
Sanders, Colonel 128
sandwich technique: rewards and sanctions 92–3
sanguine temperament 18, 19–20, 23, 28
Schachter, Stanley 50
Scherer, Christina 88
Scientific Management Theory 2–3
Sechenov, Ivan 135–6
secondary groups 53–4
Seinfeld (television series) 98
self-regulation: of activity 15–16; basis for individual strategy 43–4

Selye, Hans 34, 116–17
semantic barriers 99
sense of belonging 56
Shakespeare, William 57
signal system 20, 29n1
sitting, 137–8
skills: abilities and 37–8
Skinner, Burrhus Frederic 14
social facilitation: groups 50–2, 72
social groups: small and large 52–4
social influence 67–8
socialist realism 39
socialization: human development 49–50
social psychology 5, 10–11
social roles: groups 57–9
sociometry: interpersonal relationships 64–5
Socrates 101, 112, 122
speech, pace of 131
stability 23–5
stereotypes: human perception 130–1
Stern, William 39
stress: concept and theory of 115–17; nature of 117–18; reducing techniques 119; in work of managers 118–19
Strug, Kerri 51
stylistic barriers 99
suitability: professional activity 41–2
Surikov, Vasily 37–8
Syed, Matthew 31

talent: human abilities 37
Taylor, Frederick 2, 86
Tchaikovsky, Pyotr Ilyich 20
teamwork: groups 60; management of 76–8
technology: human capabilities in managing 8–9
tele-factor 64
temperament question 17–20, 28; four conditional temperament types 18–19; history of 17–18; temperament types and activity 19–20
theory of incompetence 56; learning about 108–9; Peter Principle 106–8
thinking, consciousness, speech: signal system 21, 28
Thompson, Larry A. 32
Thorndike, Edward 40
time management 143, 144, 145
Triplett, N. 52
twin study method: nature *vs* nurture 34–5

Ure, Andrew 2, 12n1

Venter, Craig 31, 47n1
Viteles, Morris 7–8, 12n2, 77
voice 131

walking 137–8
win-win situation: negotiating for 112–14
Wooden, John 25
words: power of 90–4, 148–50
work physiology 5, 6–7
workplace: rewards and sanctions 92–4
work psychology 5, 6–7
World Health Organization (WHO) 5
World War II 4, 59, 69

You Can Negotiate Anything (Cohen) 110

Zimbargo, Philip 68

Taylor & Francis eBooks

Helping you to choose the right eBooks for your Library

Add Routledge titles to your library's digital collection today. Taylor and Francis ebooks contains over 50,000 titles in the Humanities, Social Sciences, Behavioural Sciences, Built Environment and Law.

Choose from a range of subject packages or create your own!

Benefits for you
- Free MARC records
- COUNTER-compliant usage statistics
- Flexible purchase and pricing options
- All titles DRM-free.

Benefits for your user
- Off-site, anytime access via Athens or referring URL
- Print or copy pages or chapters
- Full content search
- Bookmark, highlight and annotate text
- Access to thousands of pages of quality research at the click of a button.

 **Free Trials Available** We offer free trials to qualifying academic, corporate and government customers.

eCollections – Choose from over 30 subject eCollections, including:

Archaeology	Language Learning
Architecture	Law
Asian Studies	Literature
Business & Management	Media & Communication
Classical Studies	Middle East Studies
Construction	Music
Creative & Media Arts	Philosophy
Criminology & Criminal Justice	Planning
Economics	Politics
Education	Psychology & Mental Health
Energy	Religion
Engineering	Security
English Language & Linguistics	Social Work
Environment & Sustainability	Sociology
Geography	Sport
Health Studies	Theatre & Performance
History	Tourism, Hospitality & Events

For more information, pricing enquiries or to order a free trial, please contact your local sales team:
www.tandfebooks.com/page/sales

Routledge Taylor & Francis Group | The home of Routledge books | **www.tandfebooks.com**